HOME

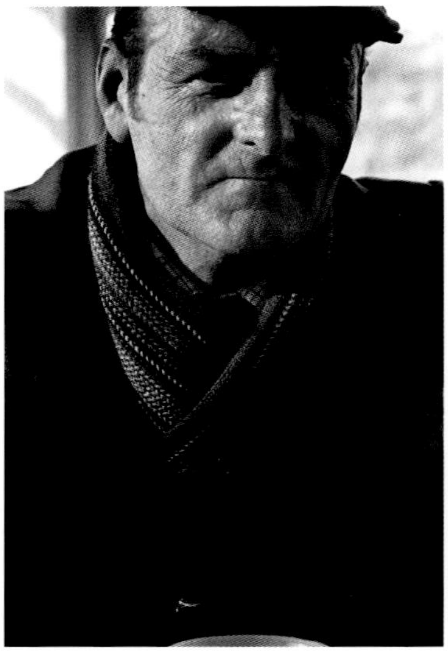

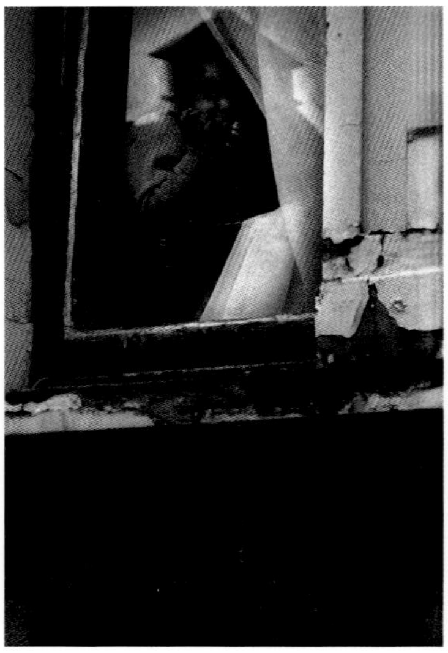

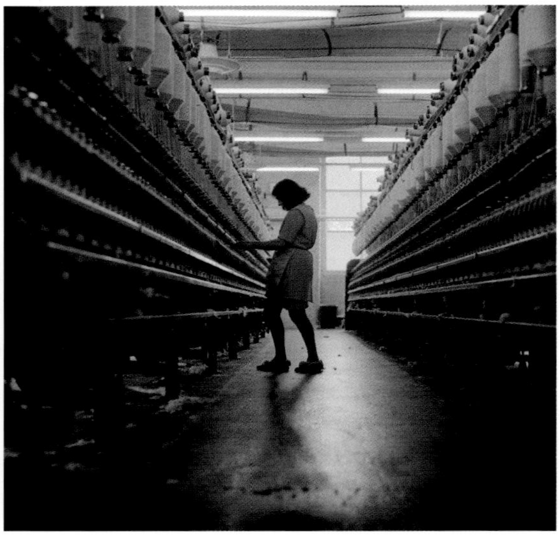

CONTENTS

FOREWORD

I was born in Detroit, the kind of place one wishes to leave. I started photographing when I was 12. I was "mentored" by the books of the great photographers. During university I became involved in the anti-Vietnam war campaign and the Civil Rights Movement. I was one of a group of students who defended Martin Luther King in a church surrounded by Ku Klux Klansmen and state troopers in Montgomery Alabama. I finished university, moved to New York three days later, got my first freelance job two days later and have not stopped working since. I moved to England in 1970. The important thing in that biography is what I call the mentoring. It was through seeing the work and reading the texts of photographers like Paul Strand and W Eugene Smith that I found an intellectual and creative home.

This background has led me to create HOME, an exhibition filled with stories from two moments in our recent past. The first period, from 1970 to 1980, is when most of the photographs in the exhibition were shot. Then I worked primarily as a photojournalist but became alienated over the use of my images. I felt art directors gave no importance to the meaning and context or to the experiences of the person who actually witnessed and made the images. I gave up working for these publications and created a children's book concept with co-author, Sarah Cox. We produced ten books in what we called the PEOPLE WORKING series. They are about what it was like to work in a car plant, on the docks, in a coal mine. They were about why trades unions were vital; they were about apprenticing, long hours, strikes; they were about the lives of working people, rather than about how to make a car or to off-load a ship.

As I worked in that decade I witnessed how the wind-down of the Vietnam war, rising oil prices and Britain's antiquated machinery, combined with a steady trickle of jobs exported to cheaper labour markets, caused rising unemployment. This was heartlessly pursued without care for the lives of the workers and their families ... I saw poverty, depression, a growing sense of futility and, along with this, the actual and existential sense of threat that customs, traditions, neighbourhoods, families, skills and trades were being lost forever. In other words I saw the destruction of all those things that constitute what people thought of as HOME.

Afterwards, between 1999 and 2004, I made 26 documentaries about food and culture around the world. I became discomfited by a memory I could not immediately place. Eventually I realised that I was seeing the same sense of loss in the eyes of the farmers, food producers, fishermen and chefs that I had seen 20 years earlier. I understood that the same processes that had destroyed British working class culture were at work again – this time destroying the economic and cultural fabric of European rural life.

Novelist and art critic John Berger said that it is imperative for art to make visible the invisible. I agree with him. I think that globalisation, and the consequent unemployment, is an insidious force like a wind arising from a distant, unknown place, a force which is all but invisible, but has a direct effect upon people's lives. This exhibition is an attempt to make that force visible.

Finally for me, photographing and filming have provided a privileged view into peoples lives and a constant inquiry into the nature of the world and into my own nature. It has been my vehicle to explore what it means to be human and in some ways to create for myself a kind of intellectual and creative HOME.

INTRODUCTION

HOME is where you come from and where you may wish to stay.

BUT

As logo-bearing products, fast food joints, tourism, movies and music travel without constraint across borders, a blanding of culture occurs in which people lose not only the sense of where they belong but the memory of belonging – the sense of HOME itself, the place which is distinctive and theirs.

Trans-national corporations impose themselves on regional markets. They move in and eradicate much of what is local and distinctive. People lose their ways of making a living; they may be forced to work for the trans-nationals or become unemployed; their community is damaged; family life is threatened; often people lose their reasons to exist. Their sense of HOME is stolen from them.

Although this process is continuous, this exhibition is about two of these periods of loss:

1. In Britain, continental Europe and the United States during the 1970s and 80s, traditional heavy industries were exported to the cheaper labour markets of the Far East and the southern hemisphere ... and workers in the established industrial countries lost their income, communities and traditions. I documented this process in England, but the anxiety and pain it caused were universal ... the American rust belt and hollow-eyed Detroit are no different from Sheffield, Hamburg or Rouen.

2. Now, global corporations are taking ever-greater control of growing, manufacturing and distributing food. Traditional family farms with their local communities, villages and market towns are being eradicated. Every day in Britain, 12 family farms close; in the United States there are now more people in prison than working the land; in India more than 100,000 small farmers who fell into debt because of this industrialisation of agriculture have committed suicide.

Between 1999 and 2004 I filmed this process throughout Europe but again the experience of loss is universal ... the empty village streets of Dorset are no different from those of Kansas or Bavaria.

Previously, trans-national corporations destroyed industrial communities. Now they are doing the same to agricultural communities.

It is these and other images and documents which create HOME ... an exhibition about the human costs of globalisation ... and a celebration of what remains to praise and fight for.

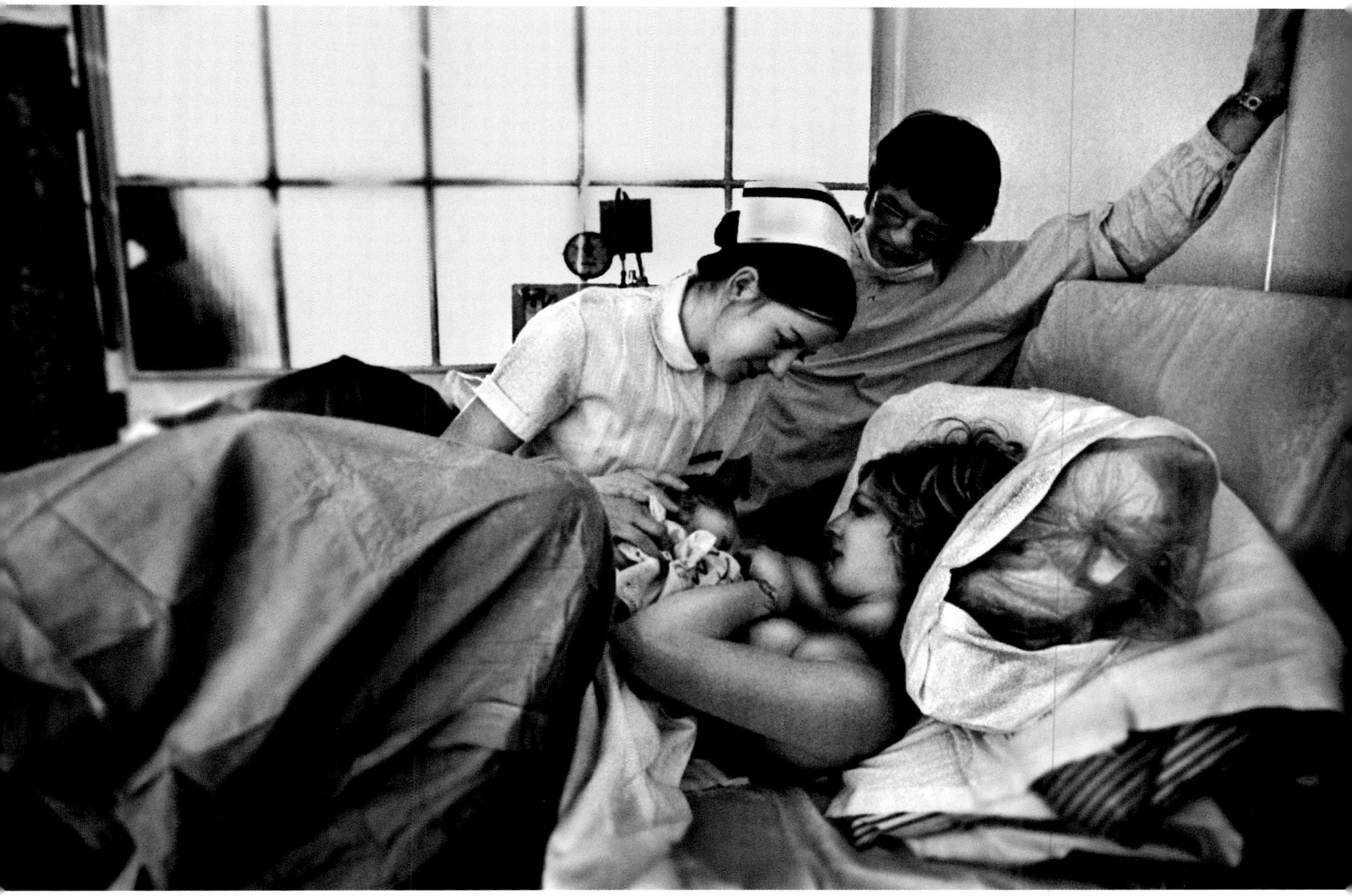

1. Moments after birth, Leicester Royal Infirmary. Spring 1977

Growing up in the Midwest as it descended into civil strife:
John Kennedy killed, Vietnam worsened, industry fled Detroit.
I discovered subject matter. I learned to see light.
Through Edward Weston I grasped that photography is a way of
understanding life as well as making pictures.
From Ansel Adams I developed a finer technique.
From Werner Bishof, Dorothea Lange and Walker Evans I detected
the ability of the medium to address social problems.

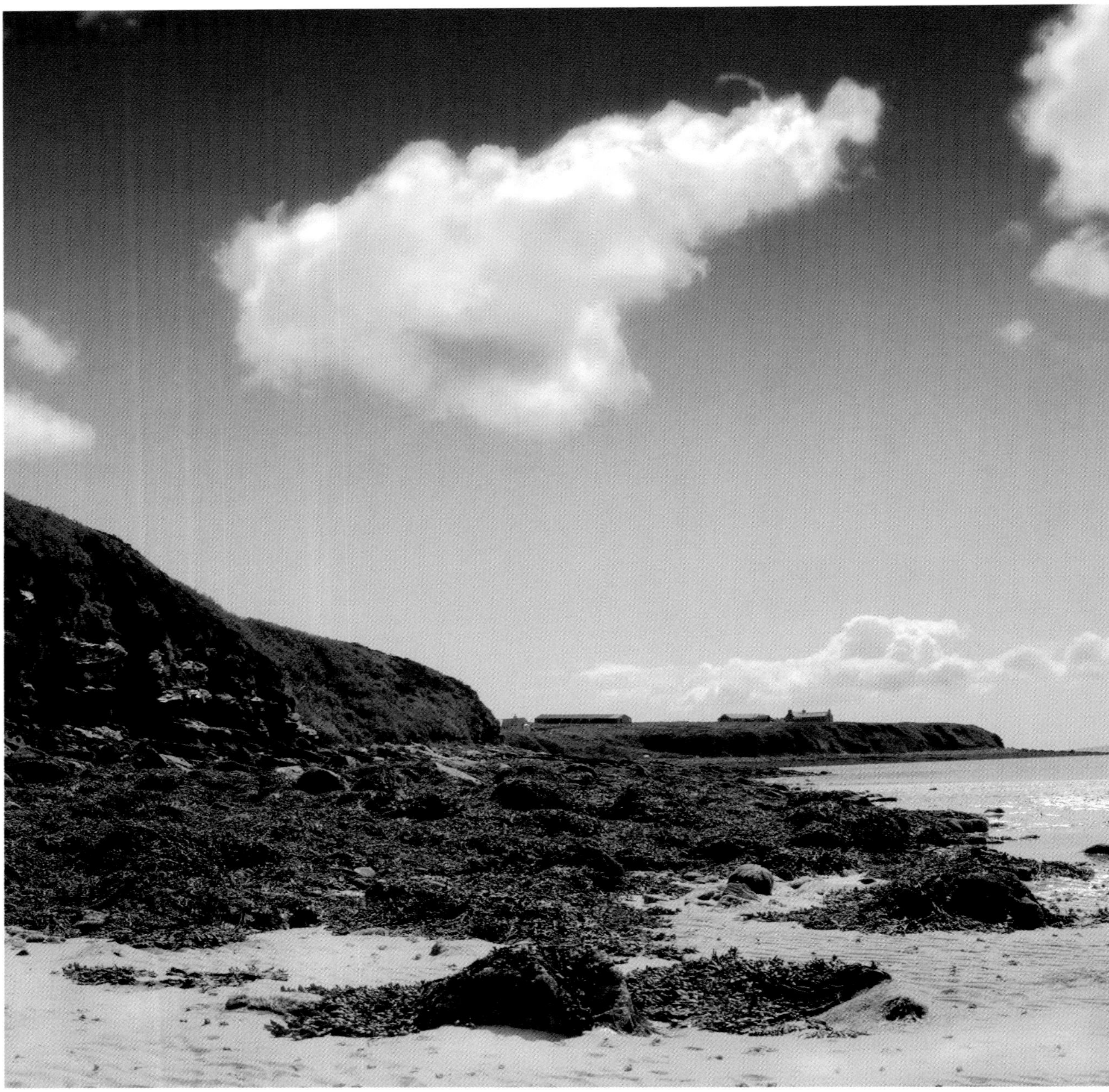

2. Rocks, beach and farm, Waulkmill Bay, Orkney, Scotland. June 2005

I screamed against destiny, trying to stop the clouds,
to freeze expressions, to hold time hostage ...
only as photography can.

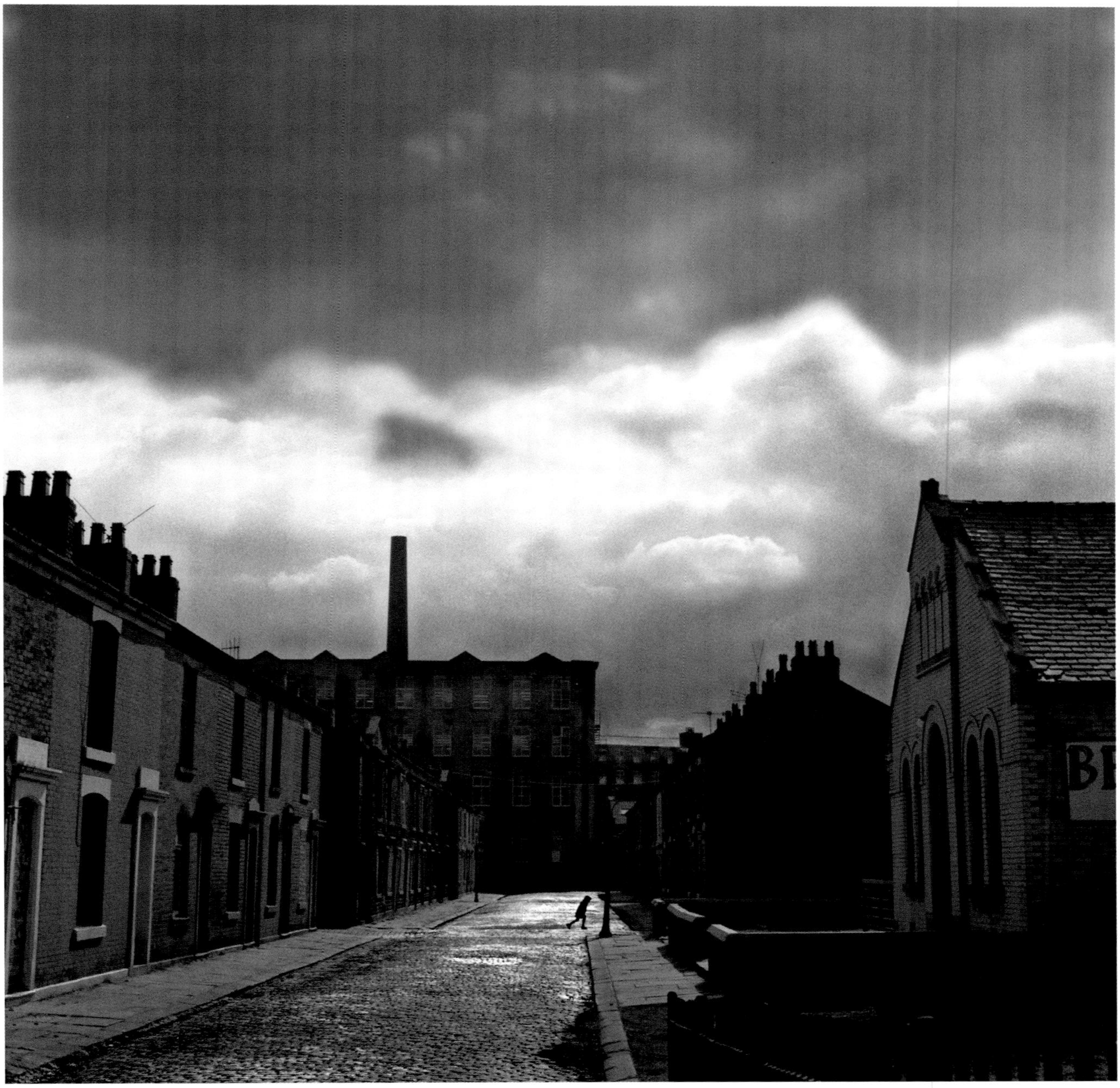

3. Blackburn mill, houses, chapel and child. Autumn 1973

I thought: "Even amateurs struggle to arrest events with their snaps,
to gain ownership over experience.
That's normal."

FARMING

OBJECTIVE:

Without agriculture we have only the food we gather or hunt. With so little wild food available we would have no civilisation. Agriculture is the activity that happens when humankind creatively engages with nature to support its own subsistence. It is another way of saying that "man makes himself". The foundation of civilised society is based on agriculture. Strange then that today it is so looked down upon, that small farmers get such a raw deal, that they are buffeted by so many laws, victimised by supermarket chains, processed food manufacturers and commodities buyers.

This is largely because the life-nurturing processes of farmers have, in the last three generations, been overwhelmed by one primary concern – to produce the largest amount for the lowest price with little regard to the nutritional quality of the food or the effects upon the earth's ecology. This leaves all other values – cultural, social, humanistic, aesthetic and health – secondary to profits and economics. It also means that nurturing, life-giving agricultural processes have been overwhelmed by the industrialisation of farming – using huge machines, depopulating the countryside, spraying our food with poisonous chemicals initially developed to kill other human beings in wars and processing the foods with chemical cocktails, bulking materials, preservatives, colourants, inhibitors, perfumes, salts, sugars, etc – in order to make nutrient-free fodder appealing.

SUBJECTIVE

A friend introduced me to the farmer who kindly allowed me to show up when I wished and to shoot freely. Over the period of a year, I, from a large American industrial city, began to appreciate the life and rhythms I encountered, along with what to me was an extraordinary thick regional accent, on the Suffolk-Norfolk borders. I have since learned a lot more about farming but then it was all an eye-opener, seeing how tough the life was, how hard people worked and how back-breaking the labour was just 30 years ago. This was an arable farm but worked in a semi-traditional way, still having animals and a few vegetable patches and fruit trees. That mixture created a life which was perhaps poorer in terms of profits but richer in terms of the farmers' connection with the land and the animals. Today, on the corporate-run agribusiness monocropped farms, the stock market is more important than stock breeding.

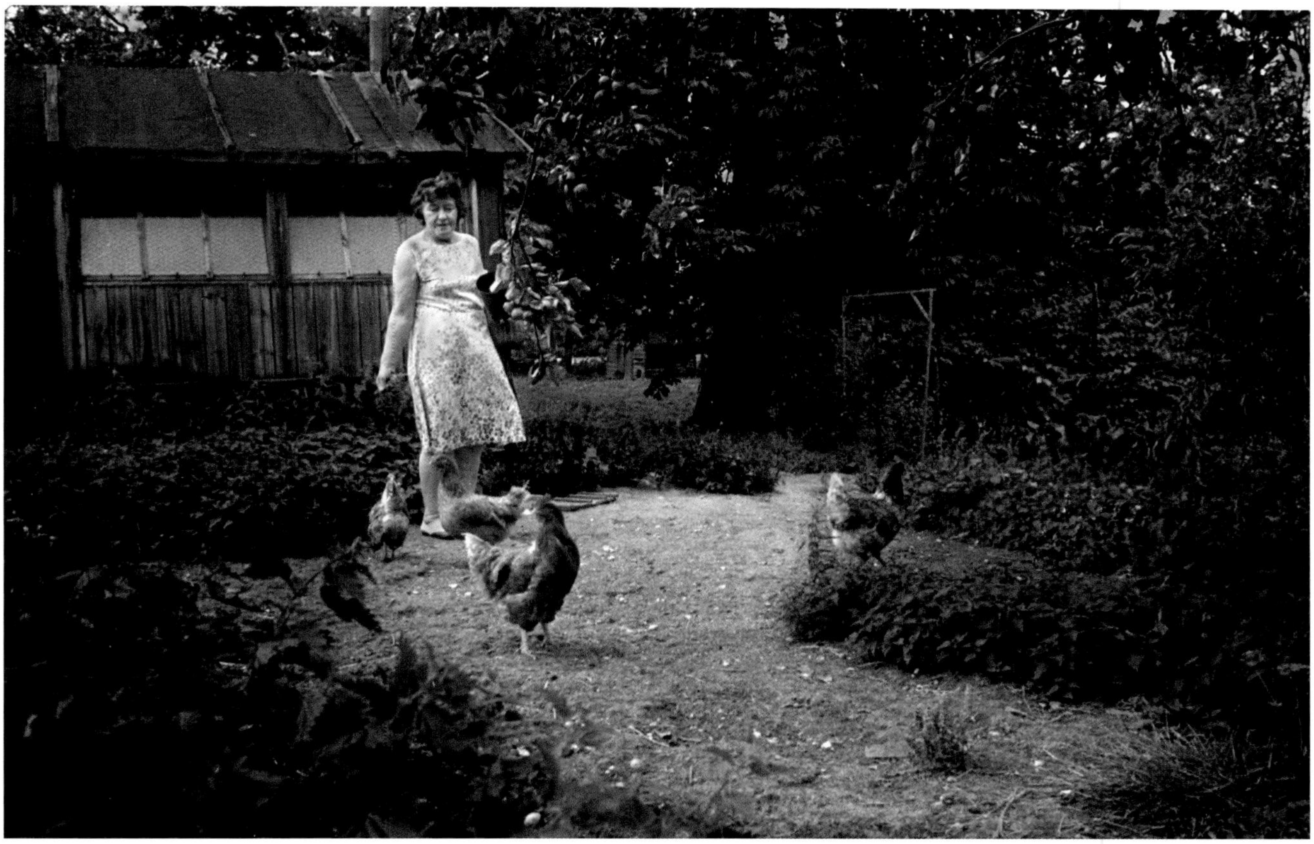

4. Farm owner's wife feeding chickens, Suffolk. July 1973

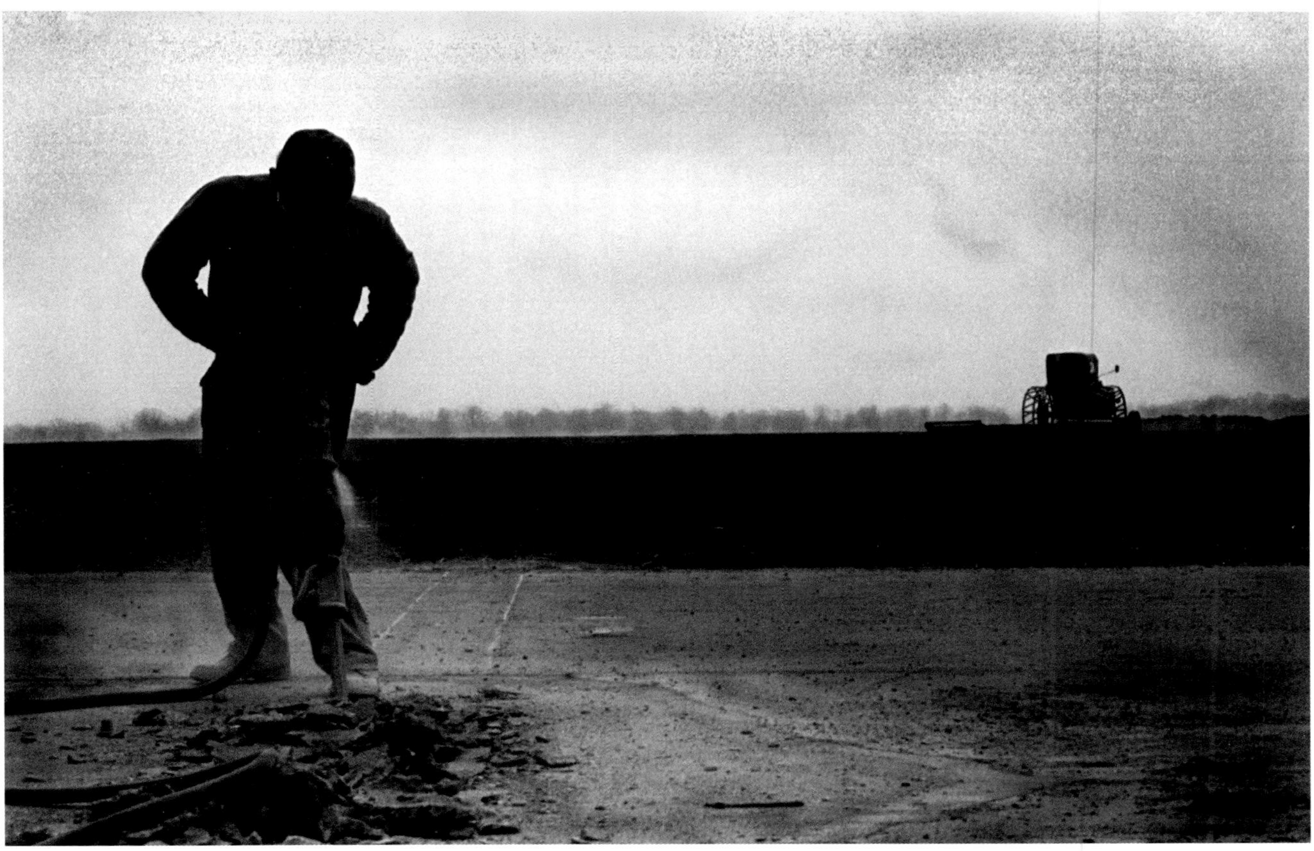

5. Farm worker drilling, Suffolk. Winter 1972-73

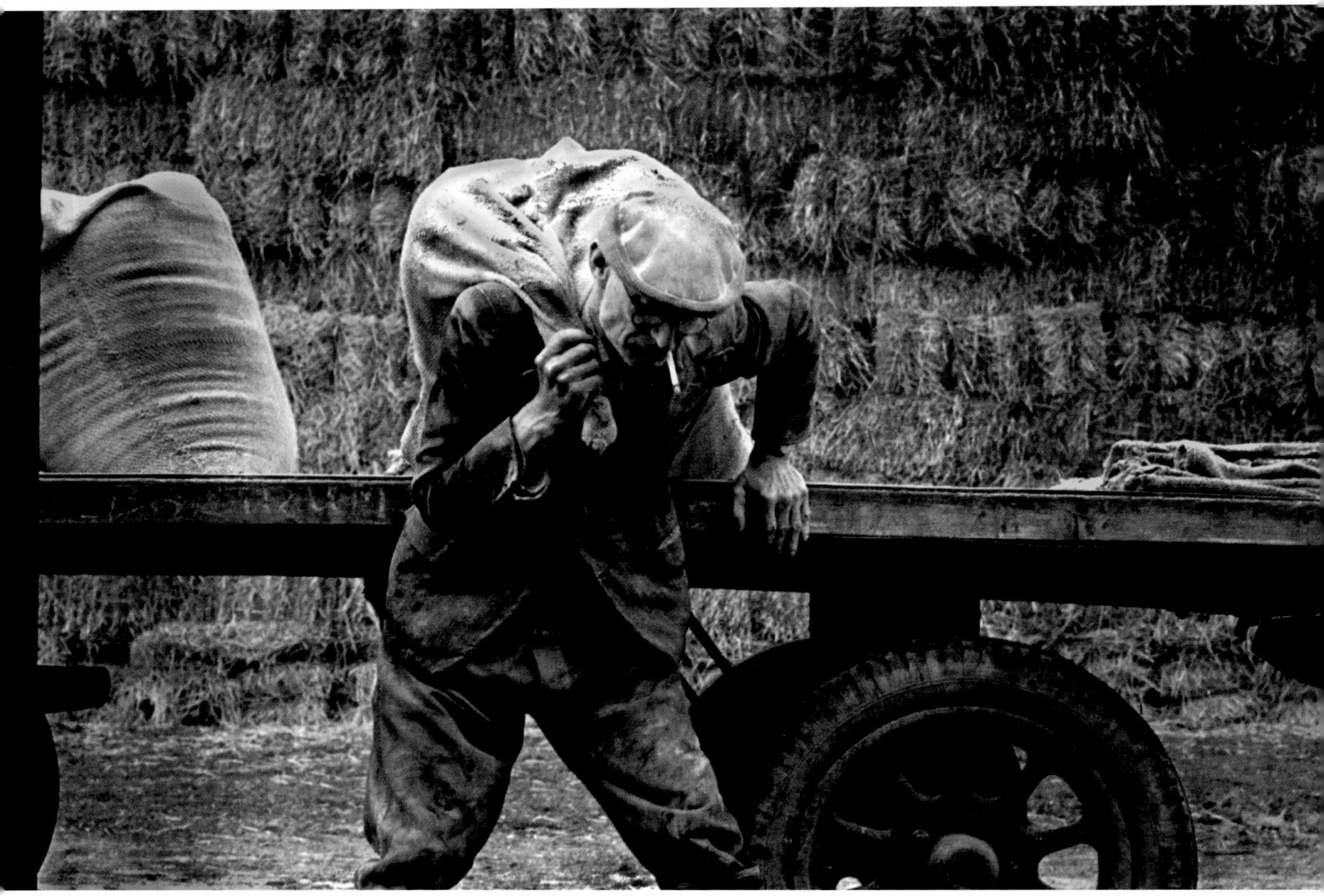

6. Farm worker lifting feed sacks, Suffolk. Spring 1973

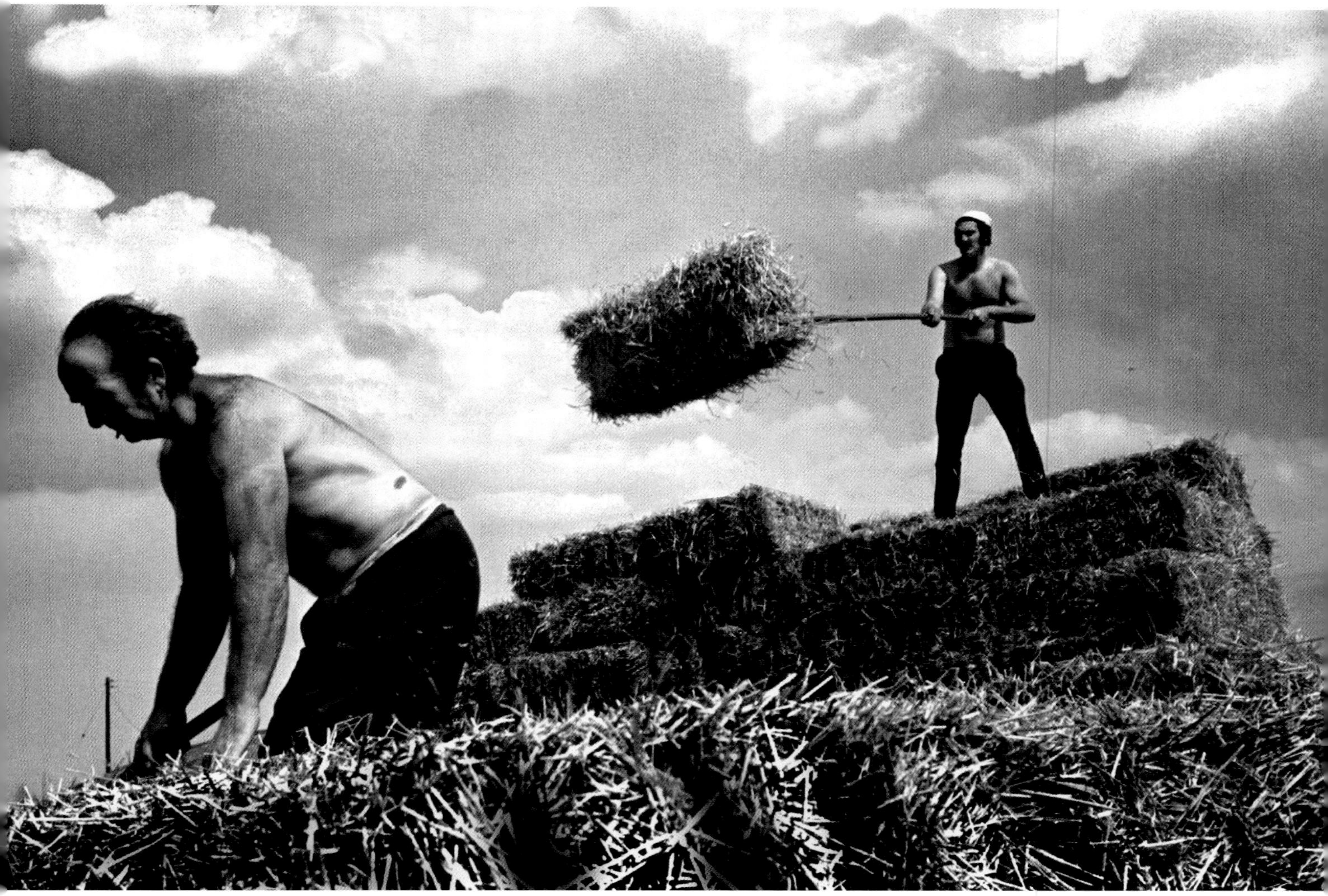

7. Farm workers stacking bales. Summer 1973

In New York city I collided with and contributed to
the counter-culture of the late 60s.
I became a professional photographer
creating experimental images
for the New York Times Book Review,
for record and book covers.
I did a story on Billy Graham, the maestro of the Fillmore East.
It was all hollow; I wondered why I made pictures.

MINING

OBJECTIVE

Extracting minerals, such as coal, from the ground is a primary industry. Without mining the rest of our complex oil and steel based civilization would not exist. Mining can occur only after growing food but before fabricating a car. In the early 1970s governments were frightened about the strength of the trades unions and in particular the power of the miners, who could shut the electricity supply down in a few weeks. The antagonism between management and the workers was palpable and continued to grow until the 1984-85 strikes against Margaret Thatcher's aggressive policies. It became clear that the Tories wanted to end the power of the unions, to destroy the centres of Labour voting and of working class culture and communities. Closing down the British mines with the rationale that Polish coal could be purchased at a few pennies a tonne less was a vengeful act that threw tens of thousands of miners and members of the surrounding communities out of work, damaged the physical and mental health of many, wiped out communities, eradicated chunks of working class culture and set the pattern for at least two generations of unemployed or semi-employed people. The union leaders warned that destroying the UK coal industry in the name of "free market economics" would lead to the country becoming dependent on foreign sources of fuel from threatening or unstable regimes. They were right.

SUBJECTIVE

I was given permission by the National Coal Board to visit Kellingly Colliery in Yorkshire. Hundreds of feet down in the winding cage, a long trek along the safe way in and finally there it was – a huge cutter protected by pneumatic pit props, slowly moving forwards under the watchful eye of an experienced miner. The noise, heat and pressure were oppressive. During a break I was told to move to the far end of the face, the side where the coal is loaded onto the underground trucks and pulled back to the extraction point. Half way across, lugging my cameras and specially encased electronic flash, I realized I was at the furthest point of safety. A moment of panic – cold sweat – and at last I got to the other side, realising that these men faced this every minute of every day of their working lives. Seeing my ghost-white face, even under the soot, a miner handed me a lump of chewing tobacco and said: "Here lad, take a chew but don't swallow, it'll do ya' good." I took it and thanked him. On the way along the tunnel, I cracked into a ripped piece of the metal sheeting that had imploded into the passage. To my regret I swallowed the tobacco saliva – but have never forgotten the kindness of that man.

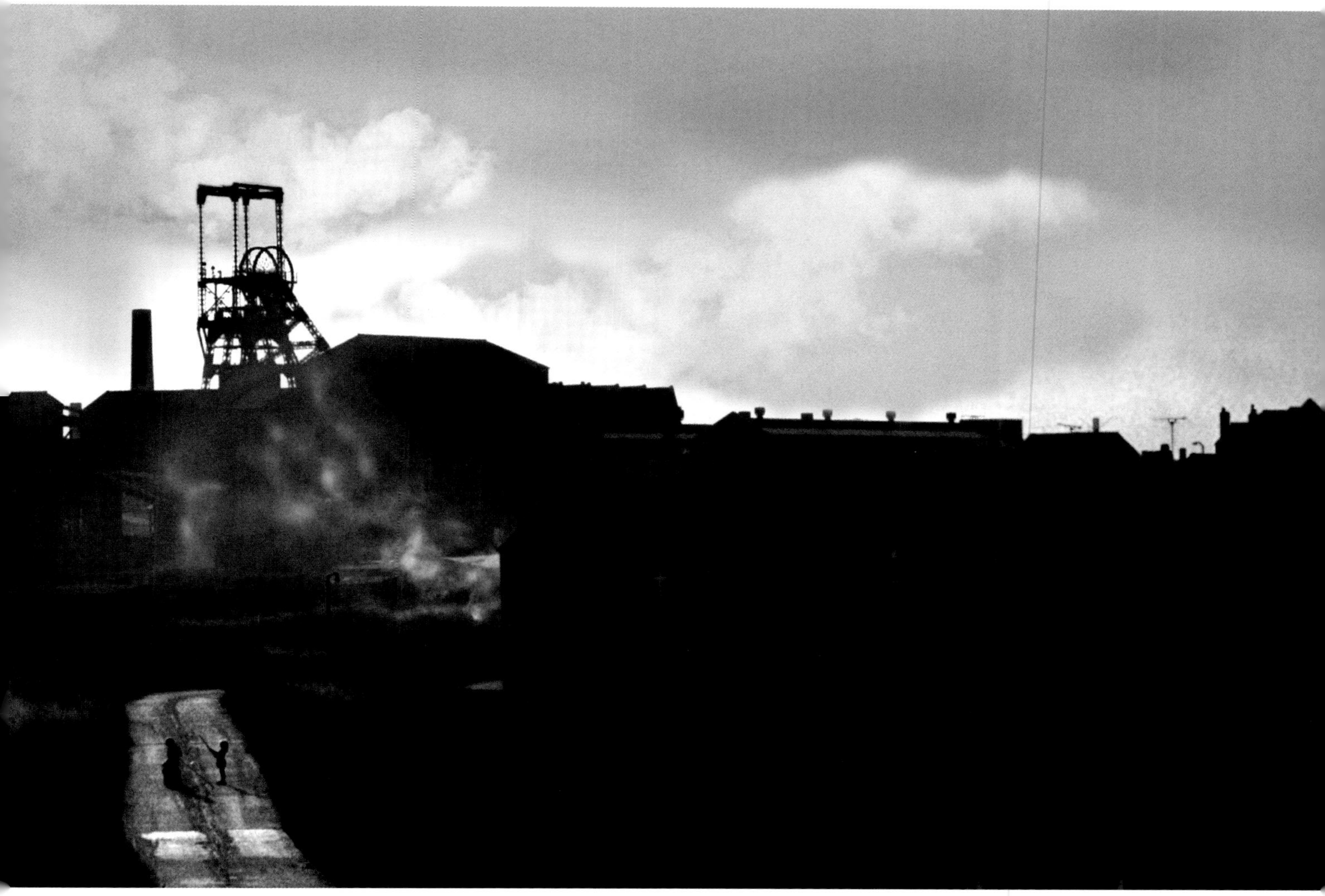

8. Kids on road in coal village, Yorkshire. Summer 1973

I knew that to photograph was to be tyrannical:
I chose the frame ...
I determined the depth and place of focus ...
I would freeze the action, or not ...
I would determine tonality and contrast ...
or determine hue and colour ...

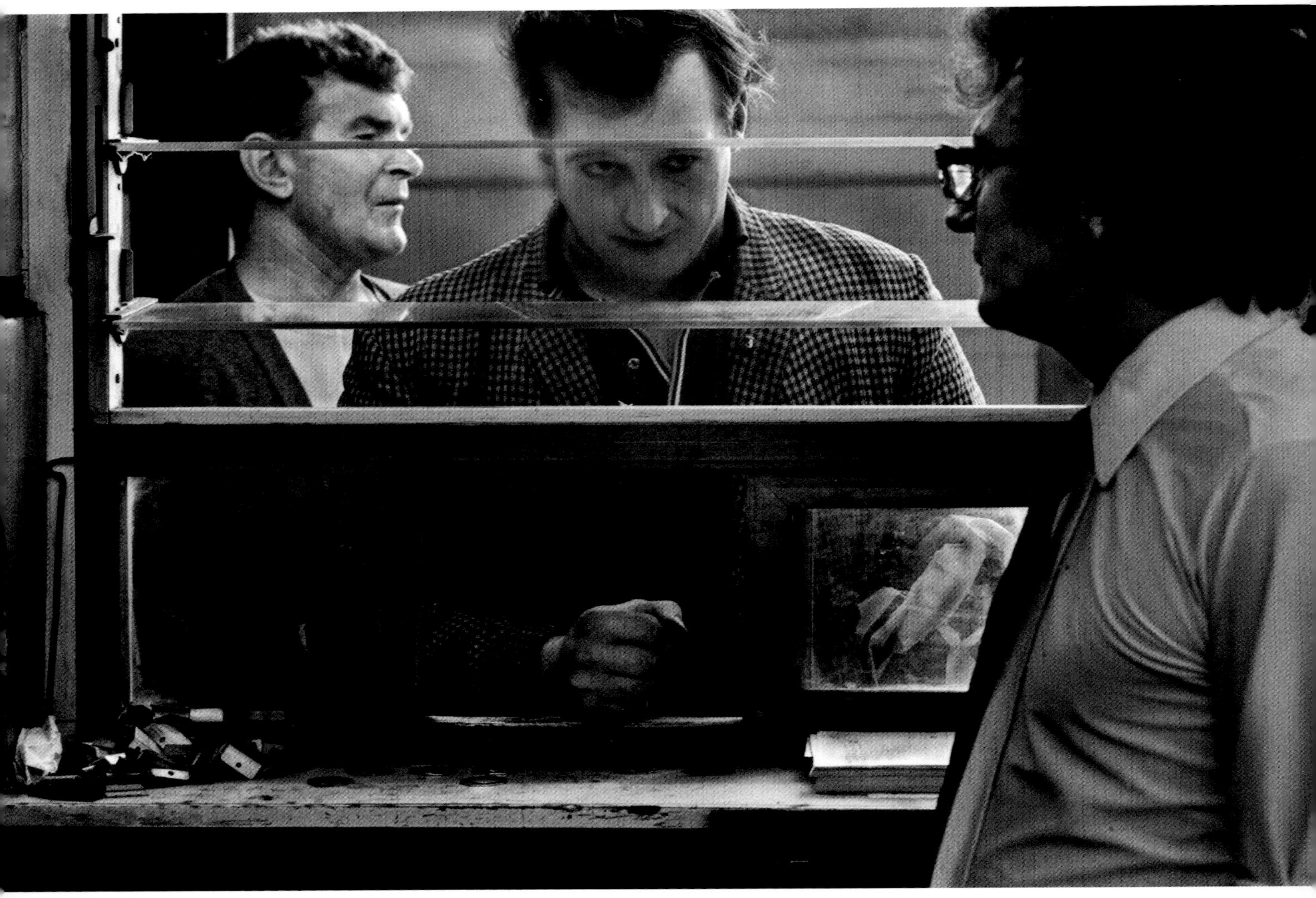

9. Argument at pay window, Kellingly Colliery, Yorkshire. Autumn 1973

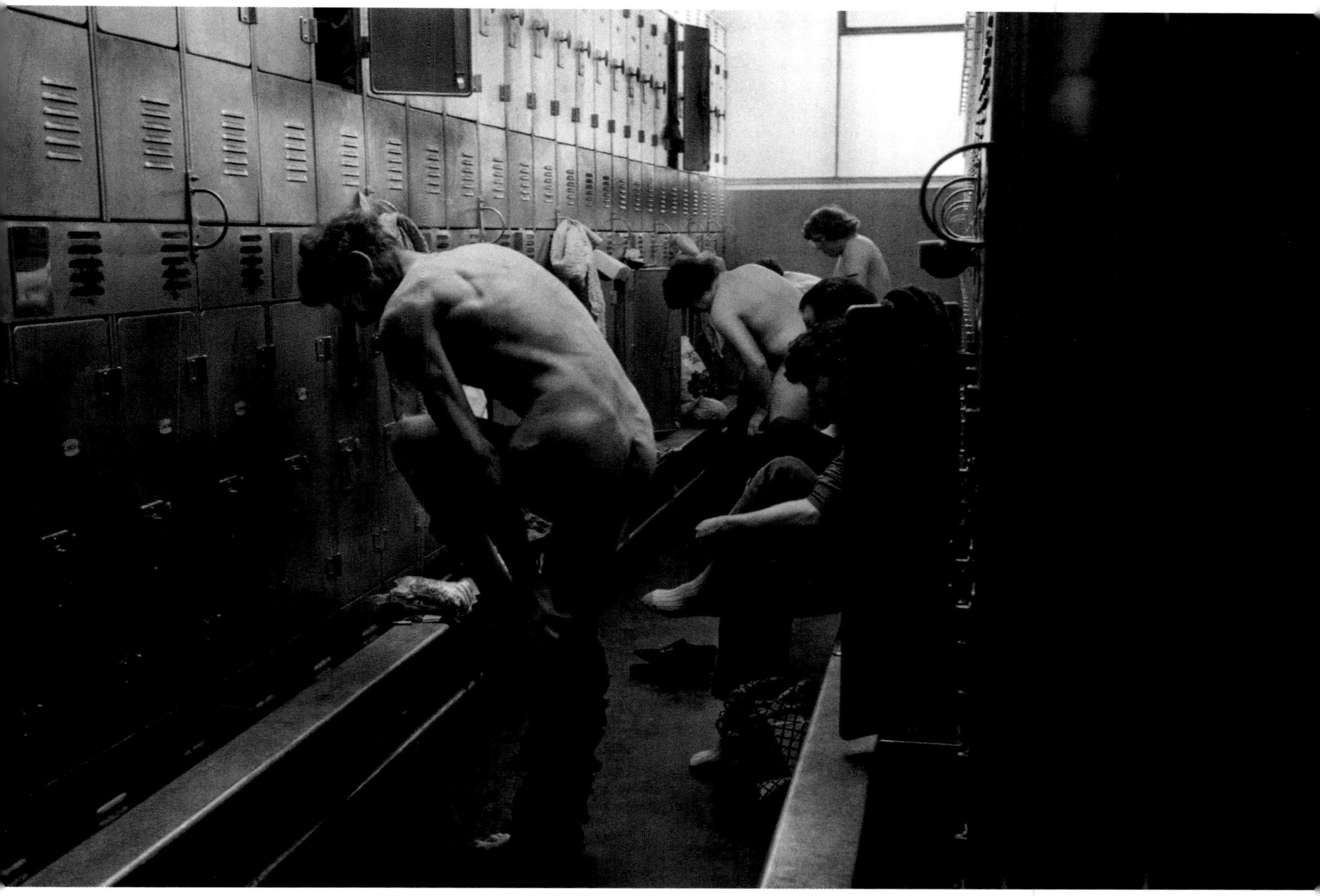

10. Miners changing room, Kellingly Colliery, Yorkshire. Autumn 1973

In the late 60s I travelled to the Southwest
photographing film locations.
Easy Rider flickered through my mind as I searched for America.
I threw it all in and sailed for Europe,
first talking to and photographing the guys on the docks.
I left to search for my cultural roots.

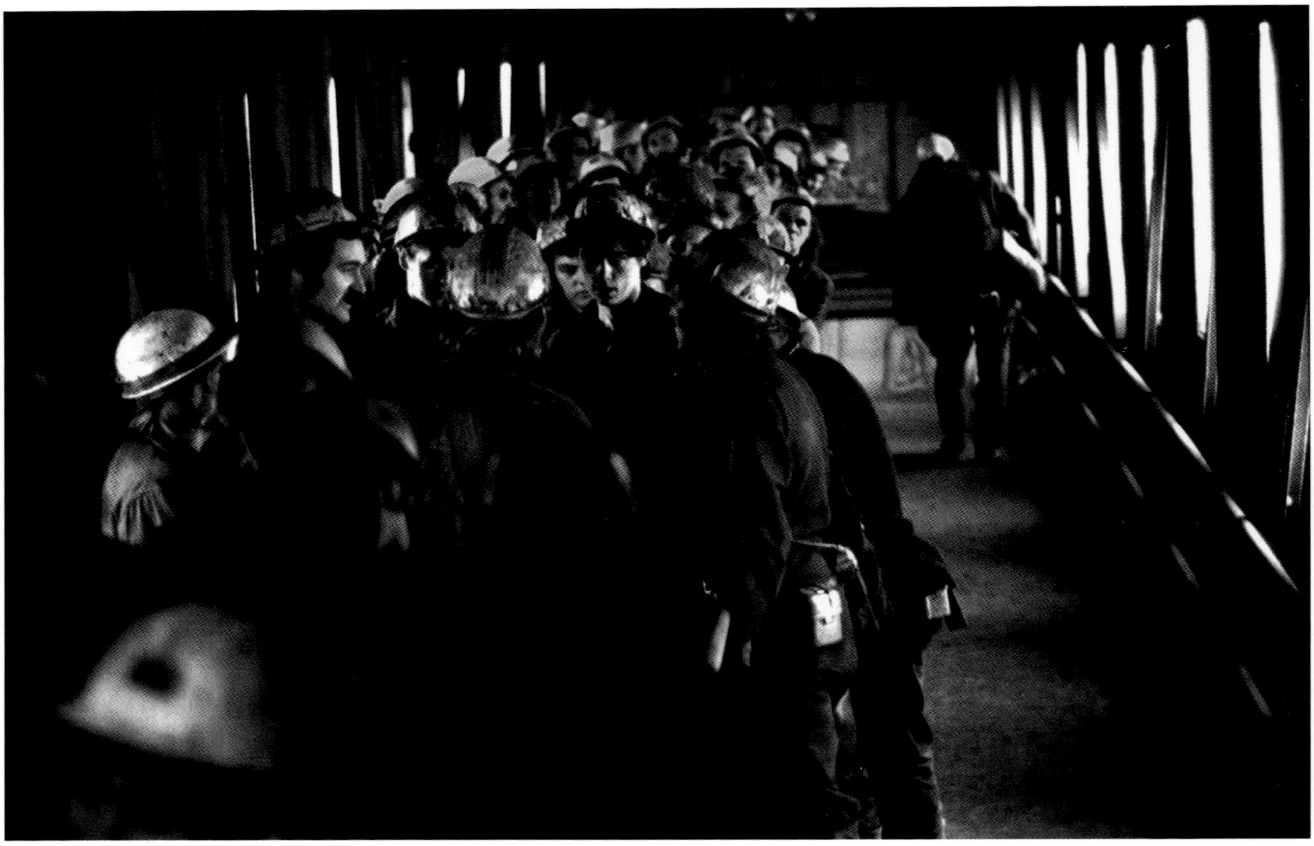

11. Miners' impromptu meeting, pit head, Kellingly Colliery, Yorkshire. Spring 1973

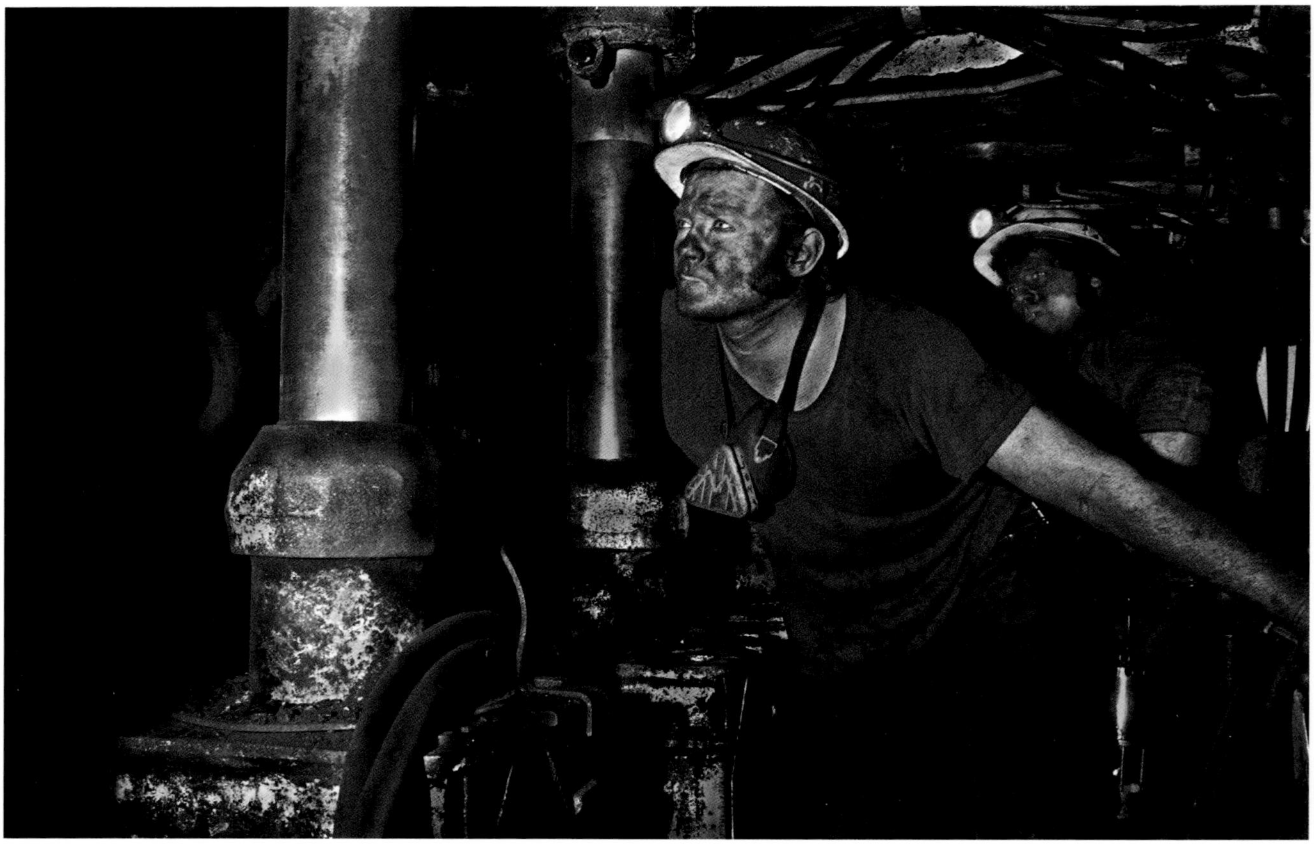

12. Miners guiding the cutter, Kellingly Colliery, Yorkshire. Spring 1973

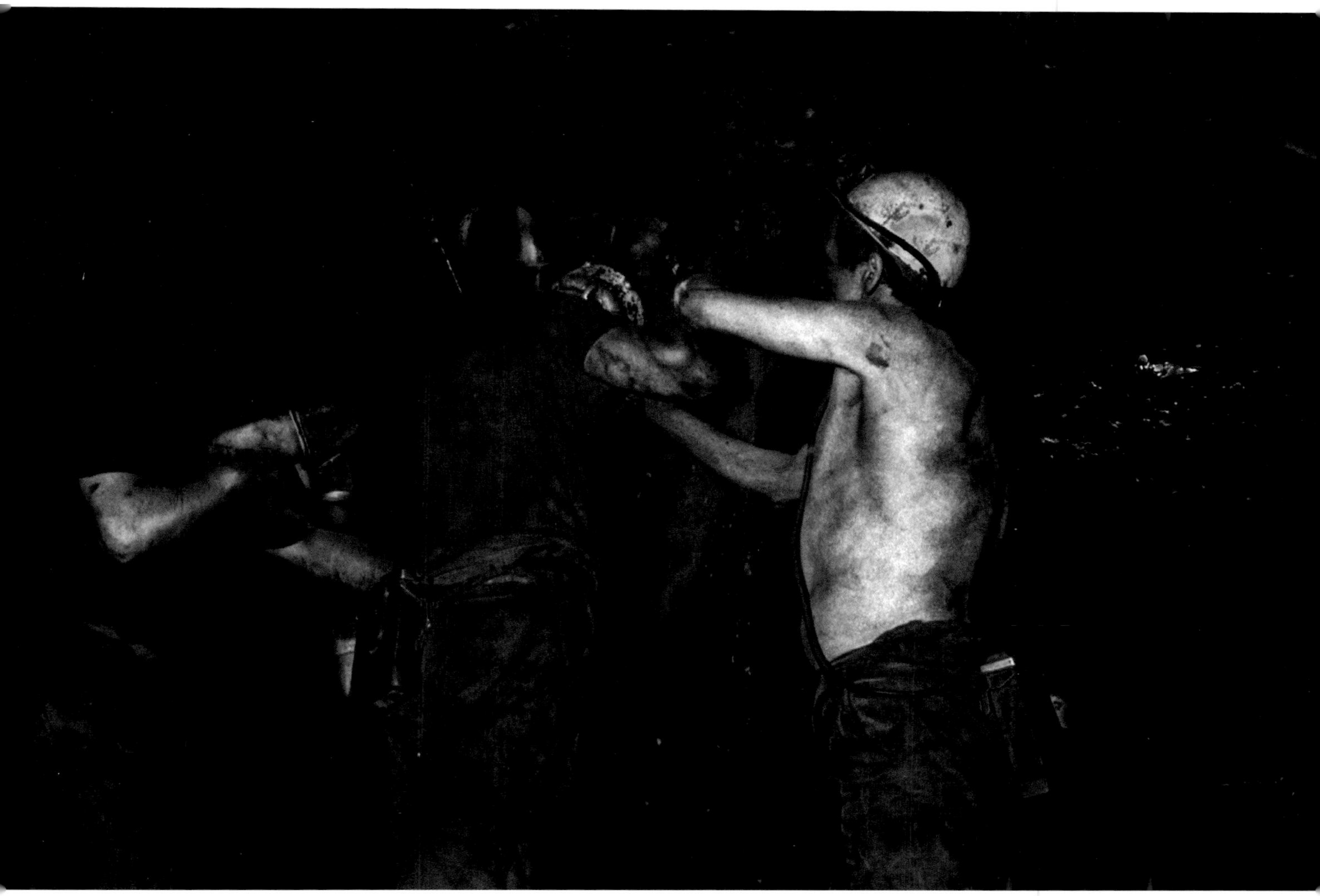

13. Dirt in the eye, Kellingly Colliery, Yorkshire. Spring 1973

In pre-hippie Ibiza I met Franco's prisoners,
I photographed under strong Spanish light
and wrote a treatise on photography
that brought me to new conclusions.

TRANSPORT

OBJECTIVE

Trade Unions are one of the great estates of a vibrant democracy. The unions must be able to legally represent the will of their members – especially the will to withdraw their labour if they cannot agree with the management. If this right does not exist then democracy is seriously eroded. During the 1970s and 80s, with a failing economy, falling employment and defensive governments, there was a fear of the great triumvirate – the miners, the rail workers and the dockers – who together could bring the country to a standstill. On the docks there still existed the piecemeal system whereby men turned up for work often to find there was nothing for them that day. Insecurity was rife and favouritism and political exclusion were practised as the men would wait to hear if their number would be called. It was easy for management to victimize outspoken workers. The dockers, like the miners, often lived in close communities with great social solidarity, a solidarity recognised by urban planners. The destruction of working class communities, explained away with the spin that new towns were being created for the workers' benefit, had more to do with politics than health. Dock work was hard and often done in sharp winds and driving rain. On the railways, men had too little time in the shunting yards to reassemble the cars for the next journey, so they would jump onto moving trains and stand between the cars to make the connections – sometimes leading to serious injury and death.

SUBJECTIVE

Many dockers have the eyes of men who constantly look over the horizon. They are removed as if distracted by a dream or more likely a worry. One freezing dawn, while I was shooting on a trawler that had just entered Hull Docks, I took a break for breakfast and entered a gloss-painted shack on the quay. As I stumbled in, cold to the bone and dangling with cameras, every pair of eyes looked at me in that unflinching way northerners have. I figured it was not going to be waiter service and excused my way through the burly men to the small window where after sufficient back and forth between my Midwestern English and the thick Humberside accent, I ordered an egg sandwich and a mug of tea. Not realizing that in this area of England I was meant to eat the "sarnie" with knife and fork, I boldly picked it up, bit into it and felt a warm glow on my hand. Looking down I realized the yolks were sunny side up, moist and leaky unlike in an American egg sandwich. I registered the faint smiles on the rest of the crew who were perhaps enjoying an anti-American moment.

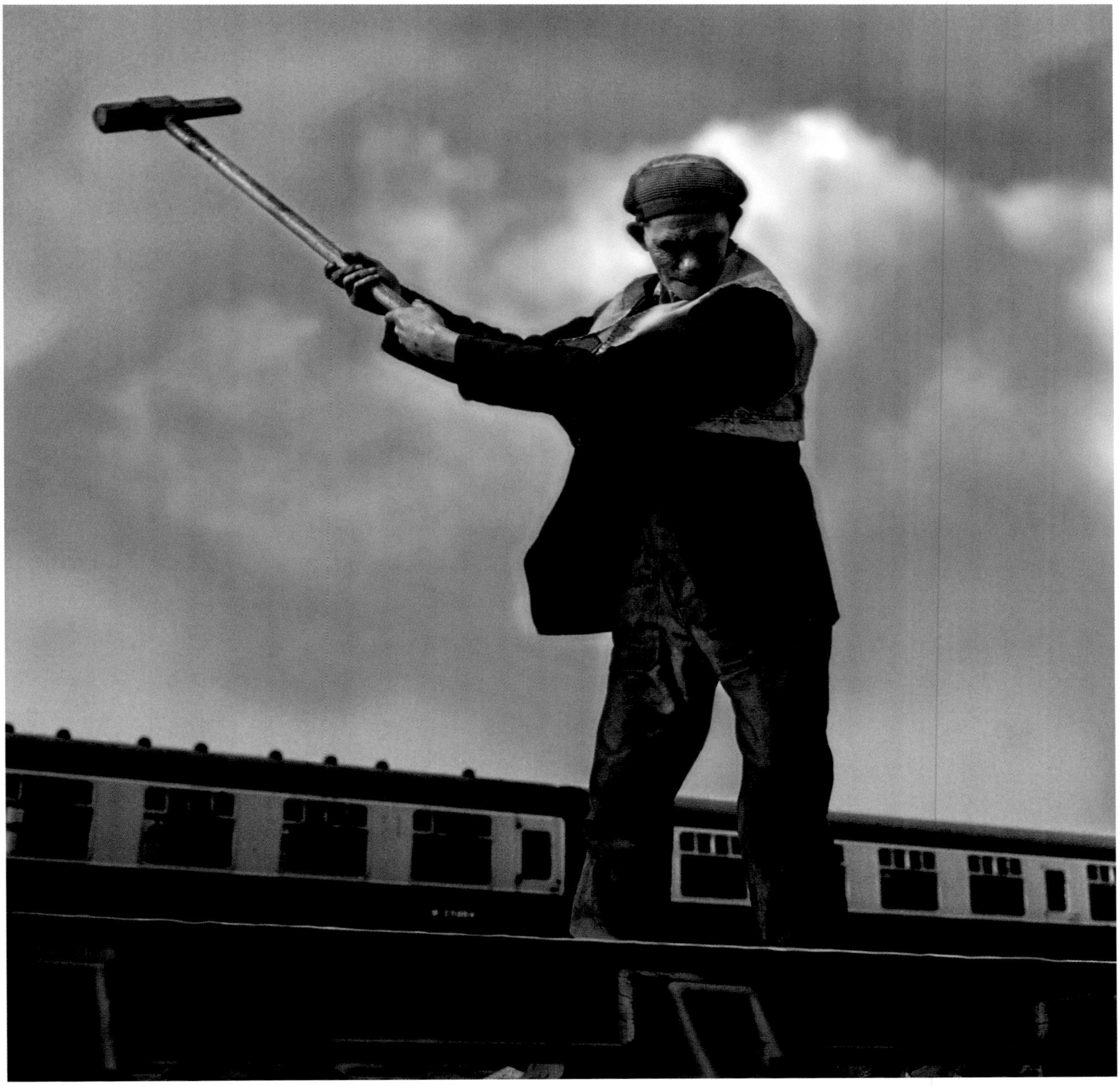

14. Rail line worker swinging the sledge, Old Oak Common, London. August 1975

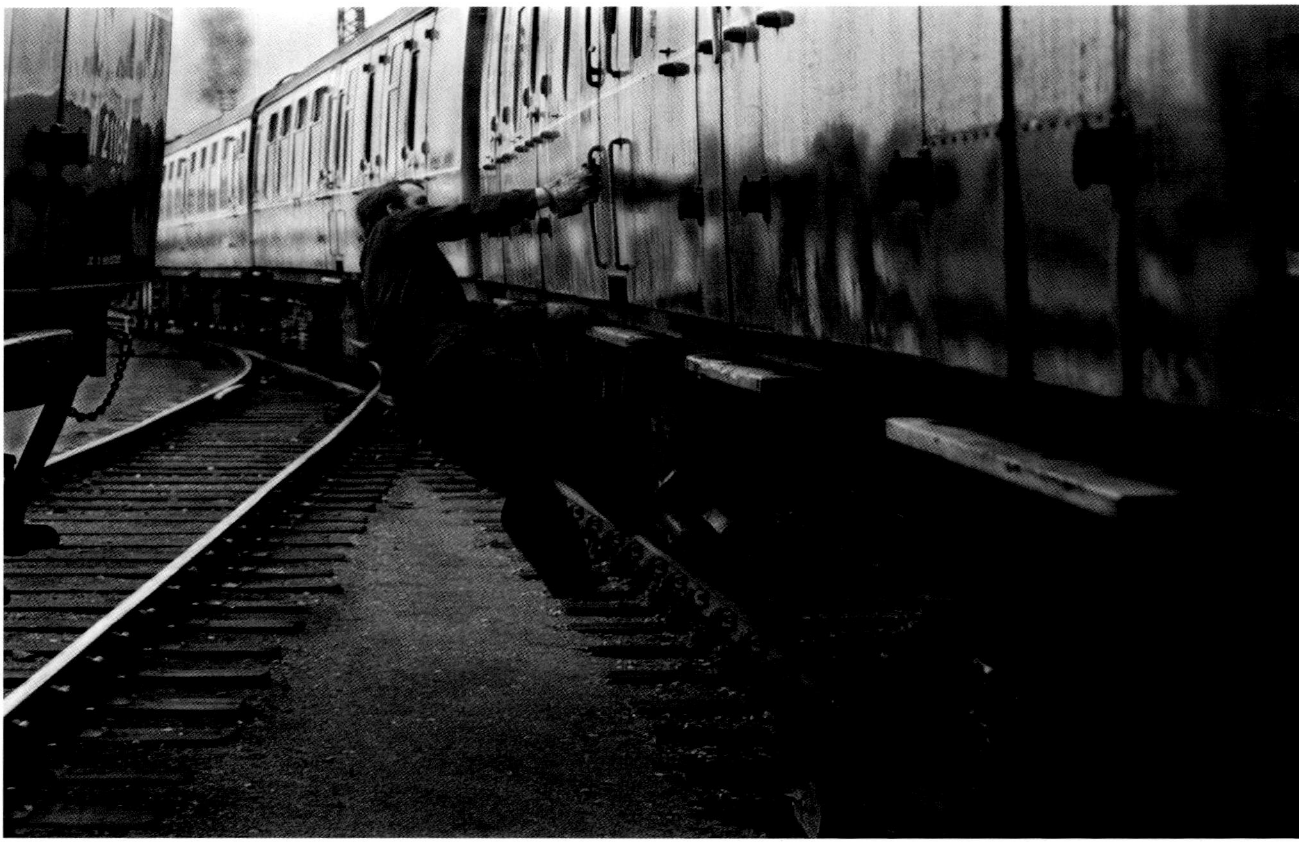

15. Shunter jumps moving train, Old Oak Common, London. August 1975

I moved to Britain. Unemployment was rising.
I devoted myself to social documentary;
I gained from W. Eugene Smith
ways of being truthful with my subject matter;
I saw more profoundly through Paul Strand the role of tones in
the "telling of the picture".

16. Exhausted shift worker, Paddington Station, London. August 1975

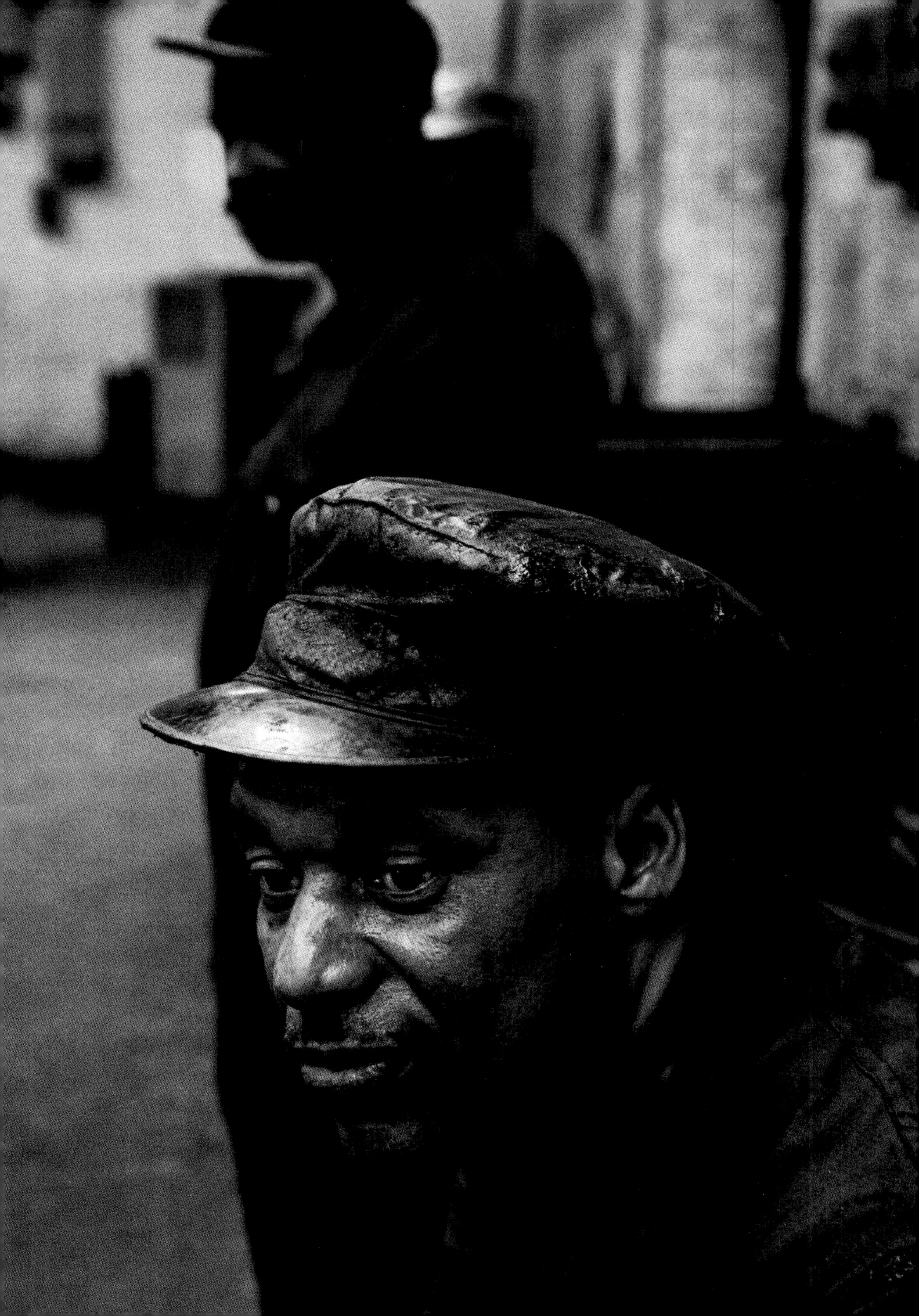

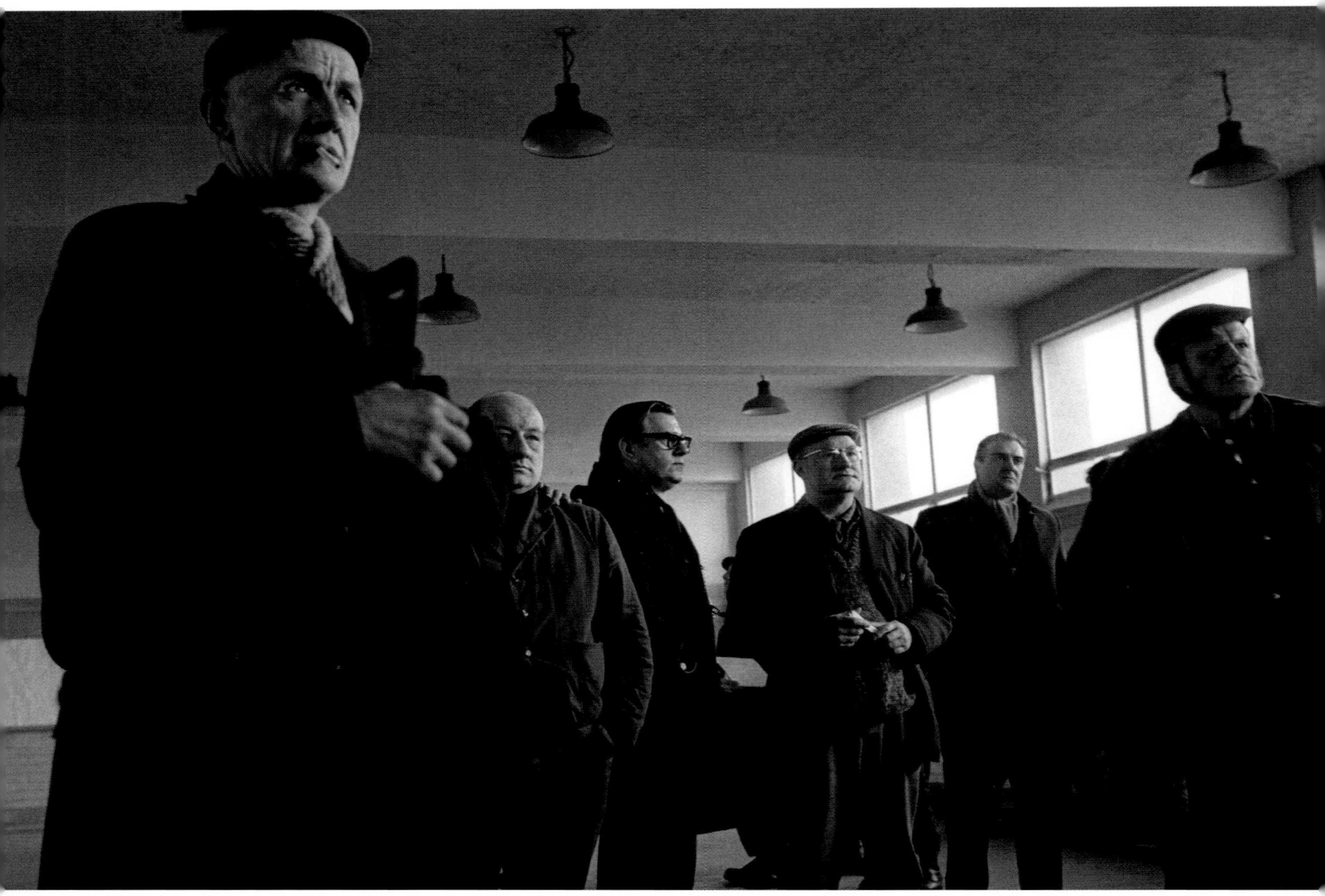

17. Dockworkers waiting for assignment, Hull Docks. Spring 1973

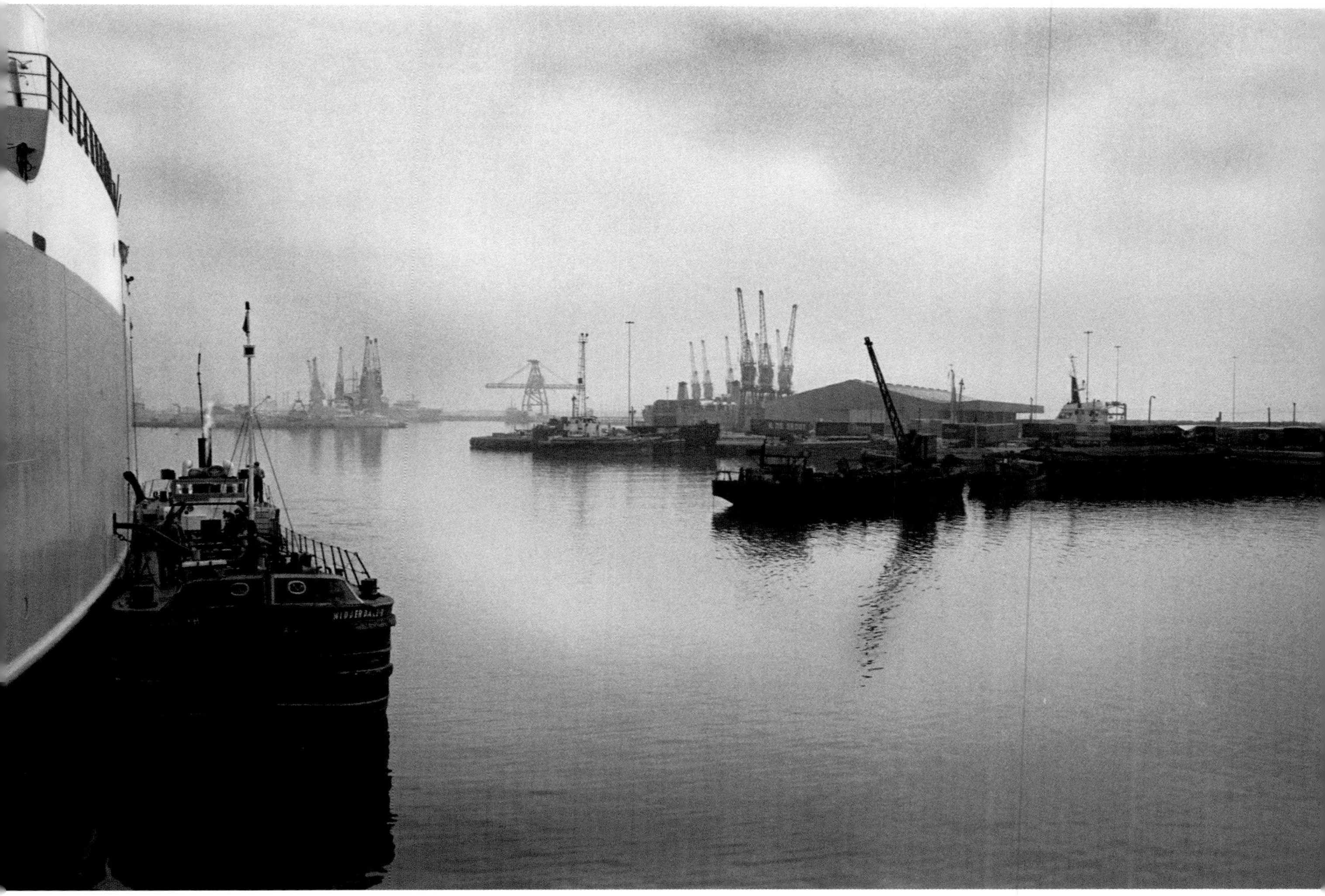

18. Barge servicing ship, Hull docks. Spring 1973

I photographed people in different workplaces
– the last moments of the British industrial working class.
I referred to the stark prints of Bill Brandt.
I encountered the mean streets of British cities.

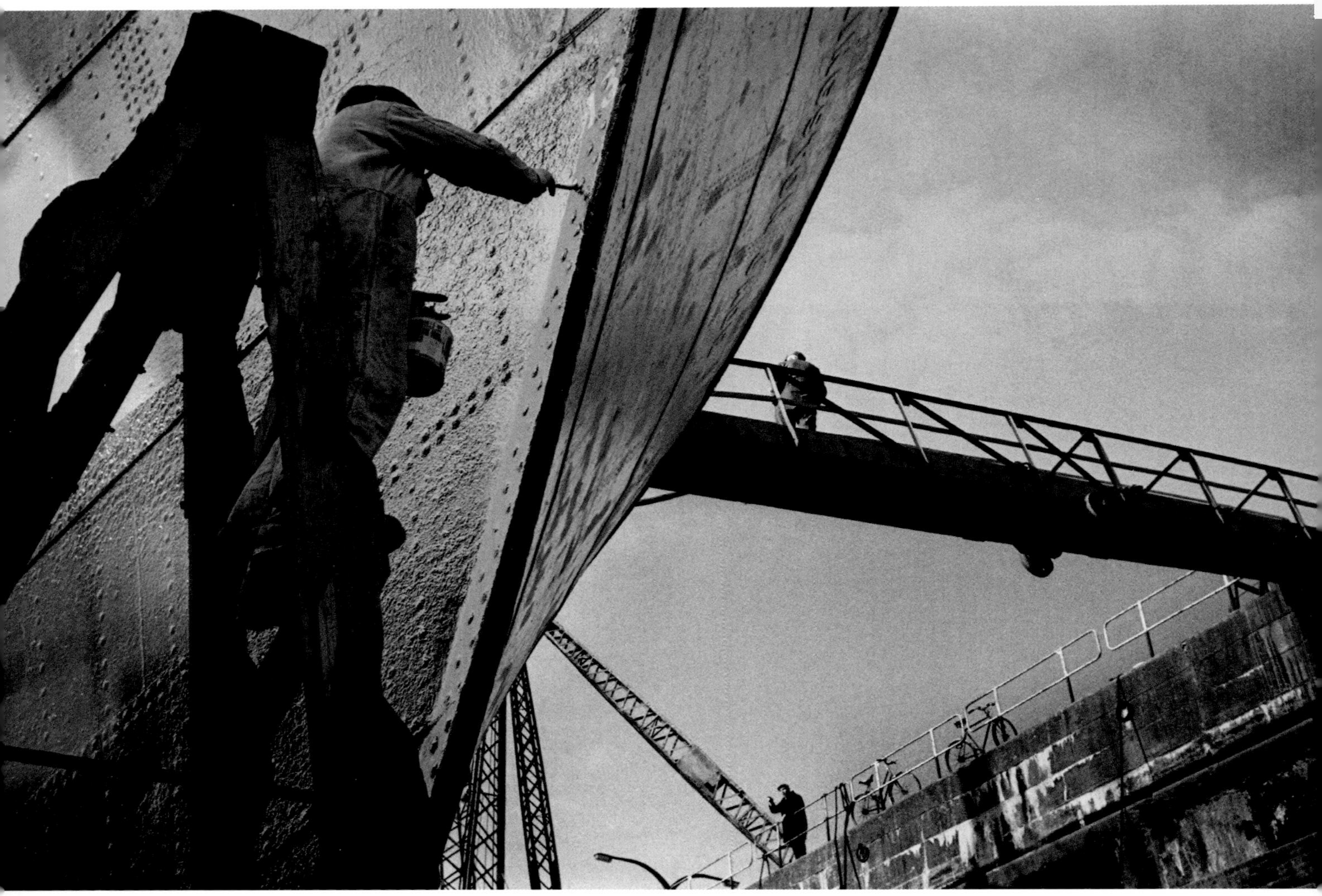

19. Drydock worker painting bow, Hull Dry Docks. Spring 1973

I photographed the Afro-Caribbean community and old age in Britain,
racial struggles, unemployment marches, street battles;
I was amazed at the ballet of violence
trapped in Don McCullen's photographs;
I was part of exhibitions in the Hayward Gallery, the Serpentine,
the V&A and around the country.
Where my exhibition about BLACKS IN BRITAIN went, riots followed.

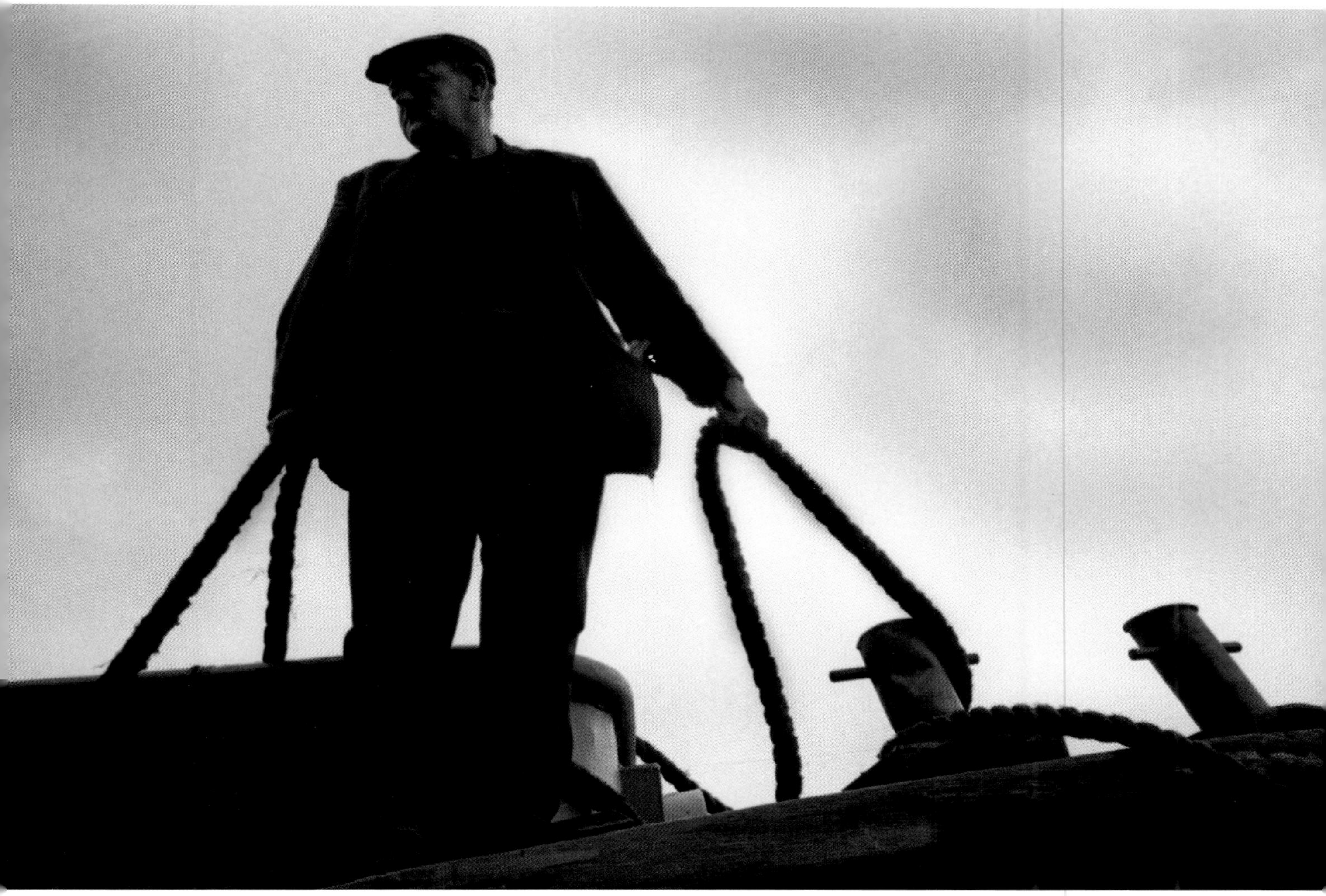

20. Bargeman, Kellingly Colliery, Yorkshire. July 1973

HEAVY INDUSTRY

OBJECTIVE

Britain created the Industrial Revolution. It was financed by raw materials extracted from conquered peoples and territories. It took place in England because, unlike their continental rivals, British scientists and intellectuals were liberated from the oppressive hand of the Church and were therefore able to think freely and to discover. They were encouraged by the Crown which recognised its best interests were to be found in mercantilism and industrialisation. Trade, military and naval superiority were understood to rely on unfettered technical development ... wealth and free thought went hand in hand. Britain maintained its technical superiority throughout most of the 19th century, but by then a new guy was on the block. The Americans had their own industrial revolution and with innovation and aggression challenged British dominance. The British responded with disdain towards the newcomer ... a mistake of manners which proved fatal. By the end of World War Two, the British managerial class was more concerned with maximising short-term profits and invested heavily in developing markets rather than renewing British industry. By the early 1970s British industry suffered from wear and tear, a lack of technical innovation and a managerial class which fostered a harsh "them and us" environment. With so many redundancies, the unions were defensive and uncompliant. Only a few years after the French upheavals of 1968, revolution was in the air.

SUBJECTIVE

Of all the places I have photographed, the car factories were the most explosive, difficult to negotiate and confrontational. Shut-downs, strikes, victimisation of outspoken shop stewards, arrests and a constant barrage against the unions by the right-wing press created a tinderbox atmosphere. Managers were concerned that Sarah Cox* and I knew too much about trade unionism and were therefore probably Communists. The shop stewards, who guided union policy on the floor, worried we might be management snoops. Once, when we convinced the stewards in an engine plant that we were okay and that we were sympathetic to their plight, the company's management assigned an overseer to stay within five feet of my every move and to have me promise not to speak to any of the workers. I was told that they were all troublemakers and Communists who constantly misunderstood and misrepresented the company's policies.

** Writer Sarah Cox and I produced ten books for children called, the PEOPLE WORKING series published by Kestrel Books in the mid 1970s*

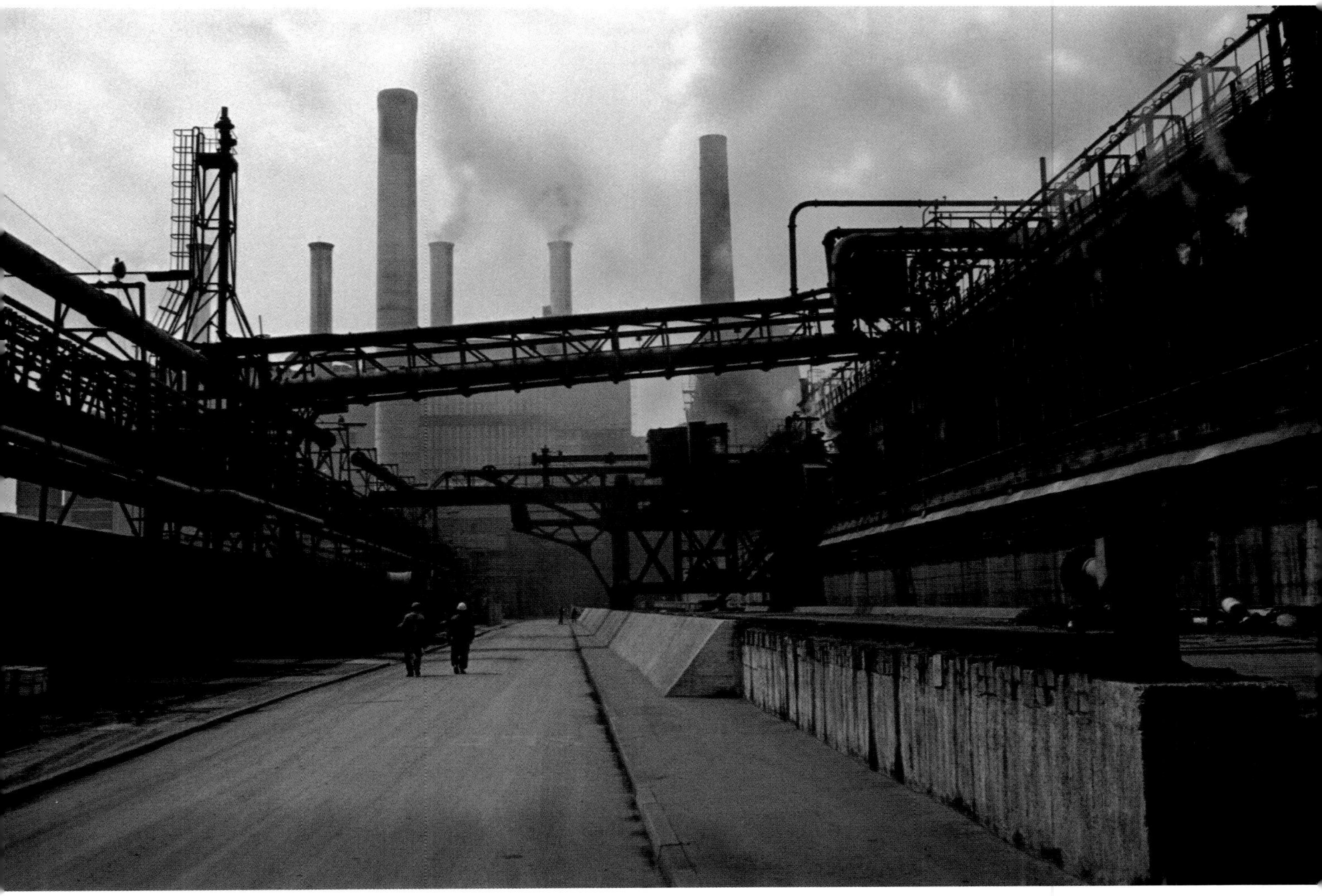

21. Car plant exterior, Luton. August 1973

I knew that whenever entering a street, a factory
or a home for the first time
I was returning to where I had never been before,
but returning, because those people,
whosoever
of whatsoever class or colour,
were a part of me.

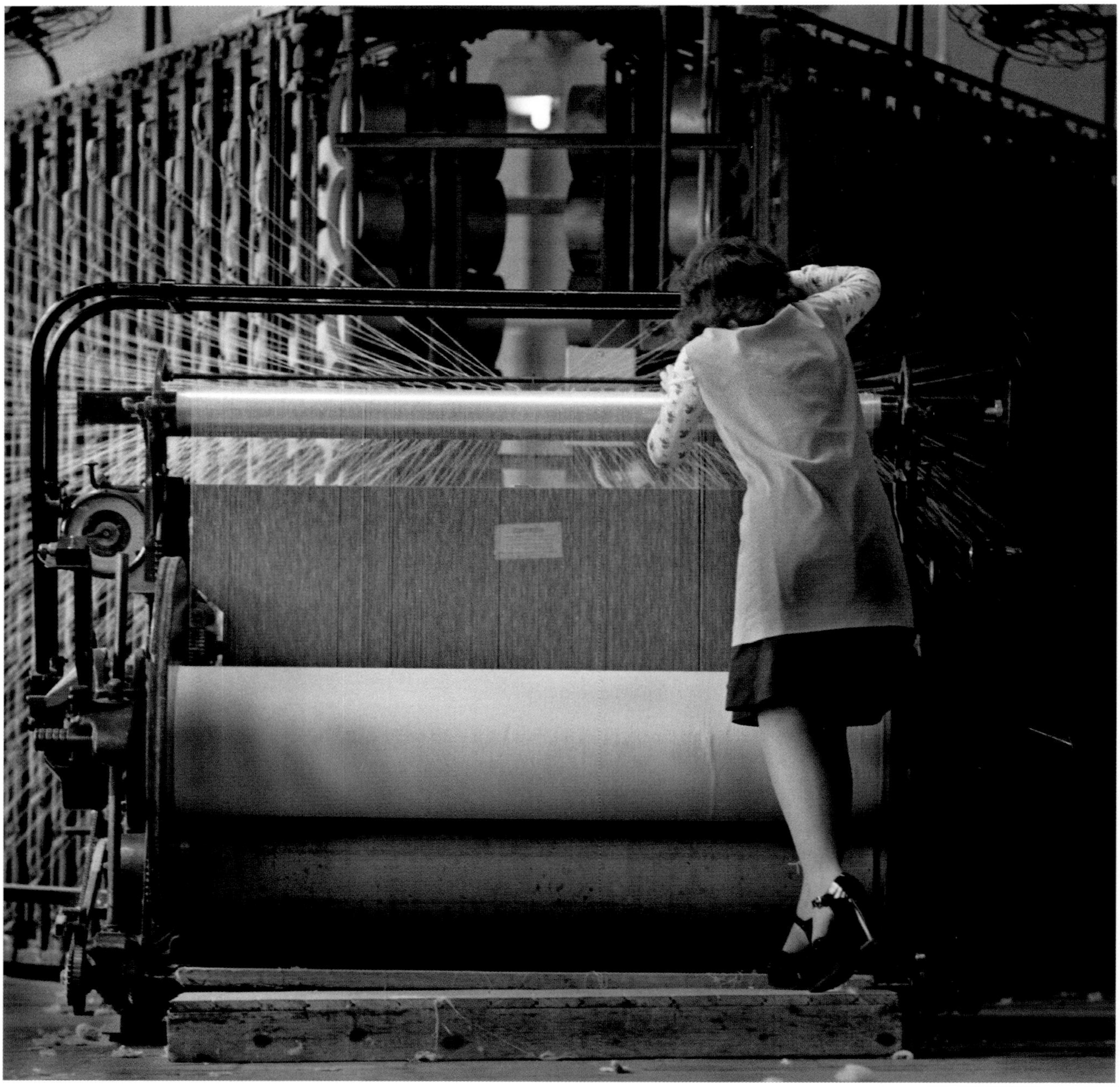

22. Textile worker guiding threads into a spinning machine, Blackburn, Lancashire. Autumn 1973

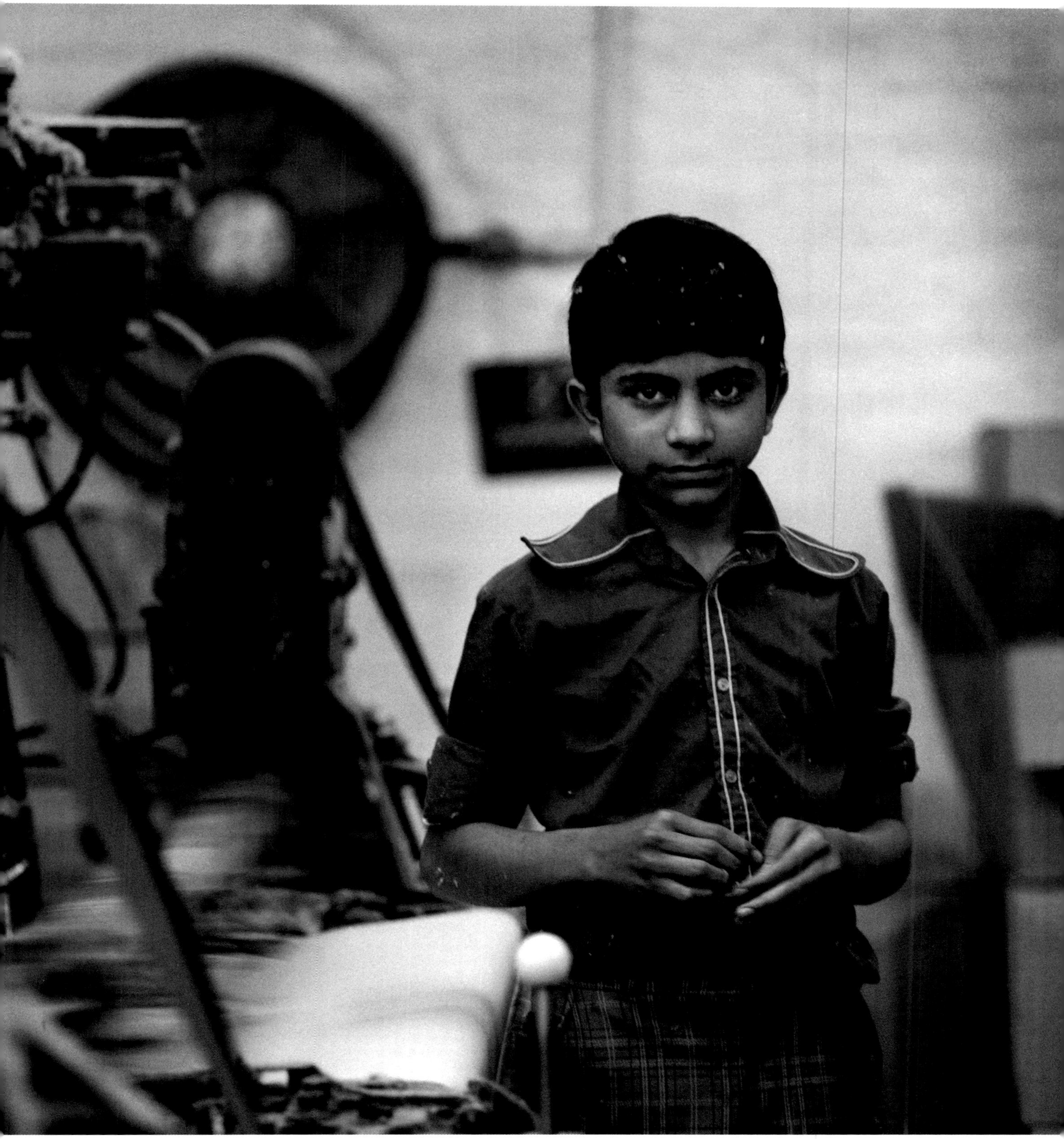

23. Child textile worker, Blackburn, Lancashire. Autumn 1973

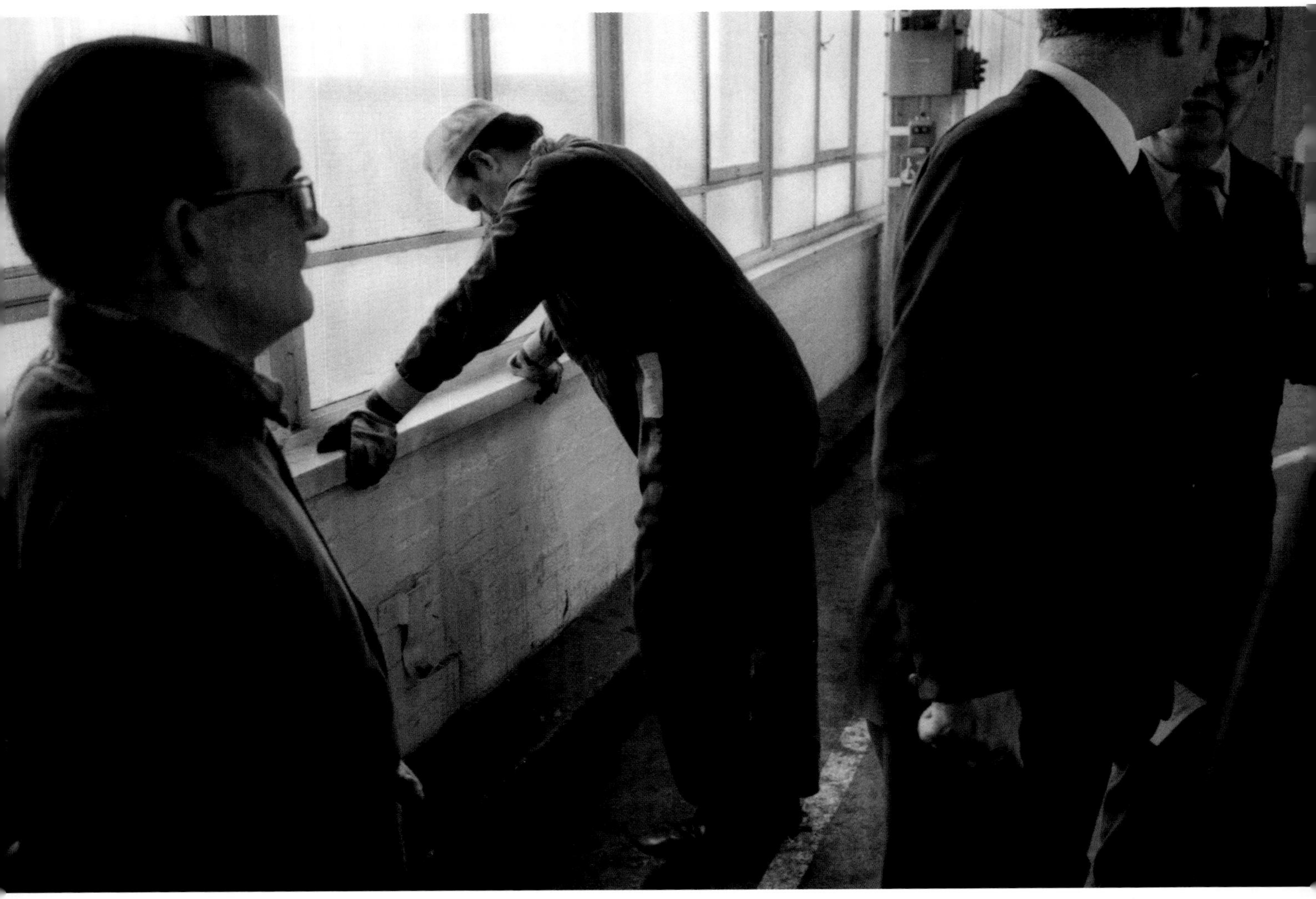

24. Exhausted spray painter, car factory, Luton. August 1973

I live neither on the surface nor inside life
as most people do.
I am a photographer, a storyteller, a visitor
I live on life's borders
with my nose pressed against other people's windows
watching, commenting, extrapolating
thinking what I think I see is truth.

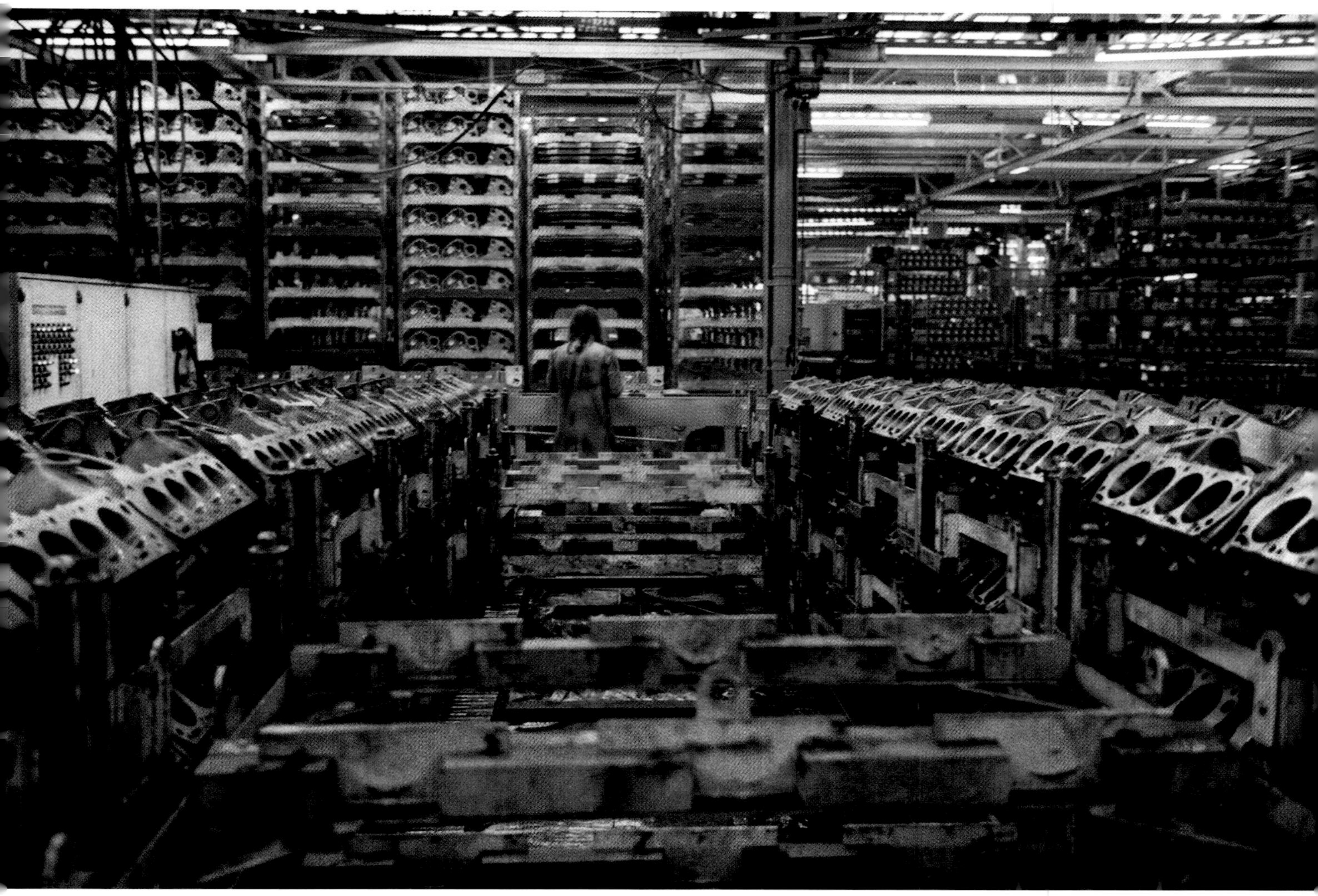

25. Worker lost in parts, car factory, Luton. August 1973

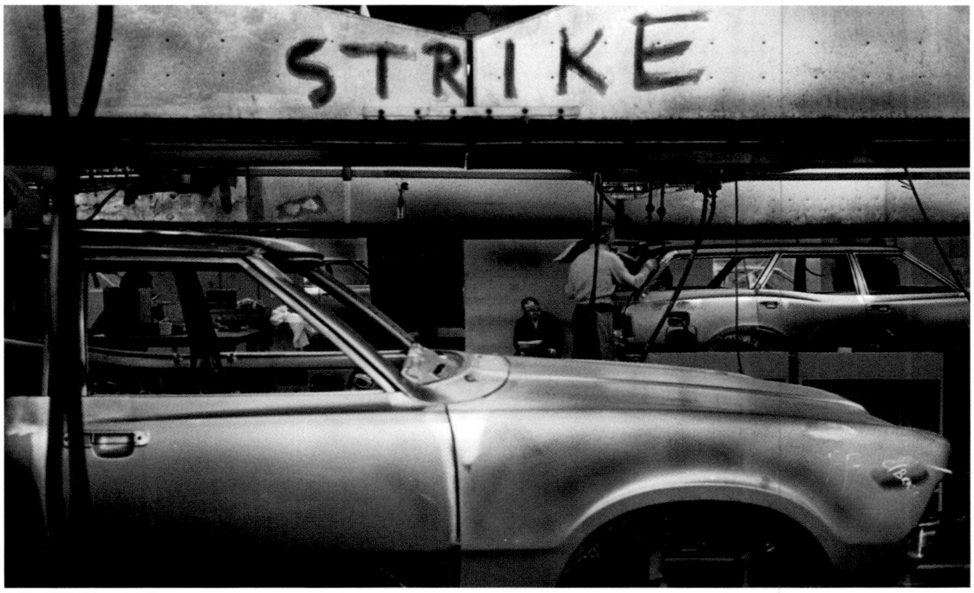

26. Strike graffiti, Dagenham. June 1973

THE INDIVIDUAL AND THE GROUP

OBJECTIVE

Communism represented an ideal that the group would take political power and control the body-politic from the bottom up. This was the dream of millions which led to a tragic failure across vast swathes of eastern Europe and Asia and in other areas of the world. It has been said that the central problem of Marxism, the ruling ideology of Communism, was that it failed to account for human avarice. After all, to rule well and maintain order, the seven deadly sins must be accounted for. It has also been said that under Communism, man dominates man, whereas under Capitalism (or the free market as it is called today) it is just the opposite. Within European social democracy, politicians often succumb to the pressures of big business and especially to the ever-growing pressures of the trans-national corporations that wield such control over wealth production and job creation. But there is also a moral disposition towards lifting the poor out of poverty, creating decent public services and providing education to ever-wider sectors of the population. Under Thatcher in the UK, there was a politically-led shift away from the concepts of social democracy towards an unforgiving, American-style democracy, where the myth of the individual over-rules the principles of collectivity. Thatcherism led people to believe that being a consumer was more important than being a producer. It created an environment for psychology to replace history as a way of understanding ourselves. It loosened the traditional bond between rights as an individual and responsibility as a citizen.

SUBJECTIVE

As a photographer and a film maker, it has been clear to me, time after time, the greater the sense of local solidarity the more welcoming and less suspicious people have been towards me as an inquiring outsider. When I was first in Britain and travelling around photographing, I noticed that the further I went into the heartlands of the industrial working class, the more generous and warm were the people. I believe that the very act of having to rely on the person next to you in a production process, especially when it effects your wellbeing and safety, creates a natural tendency towards social solidarity, tolerance and acceptance

27. Young man, Brixton Market, London. 1978

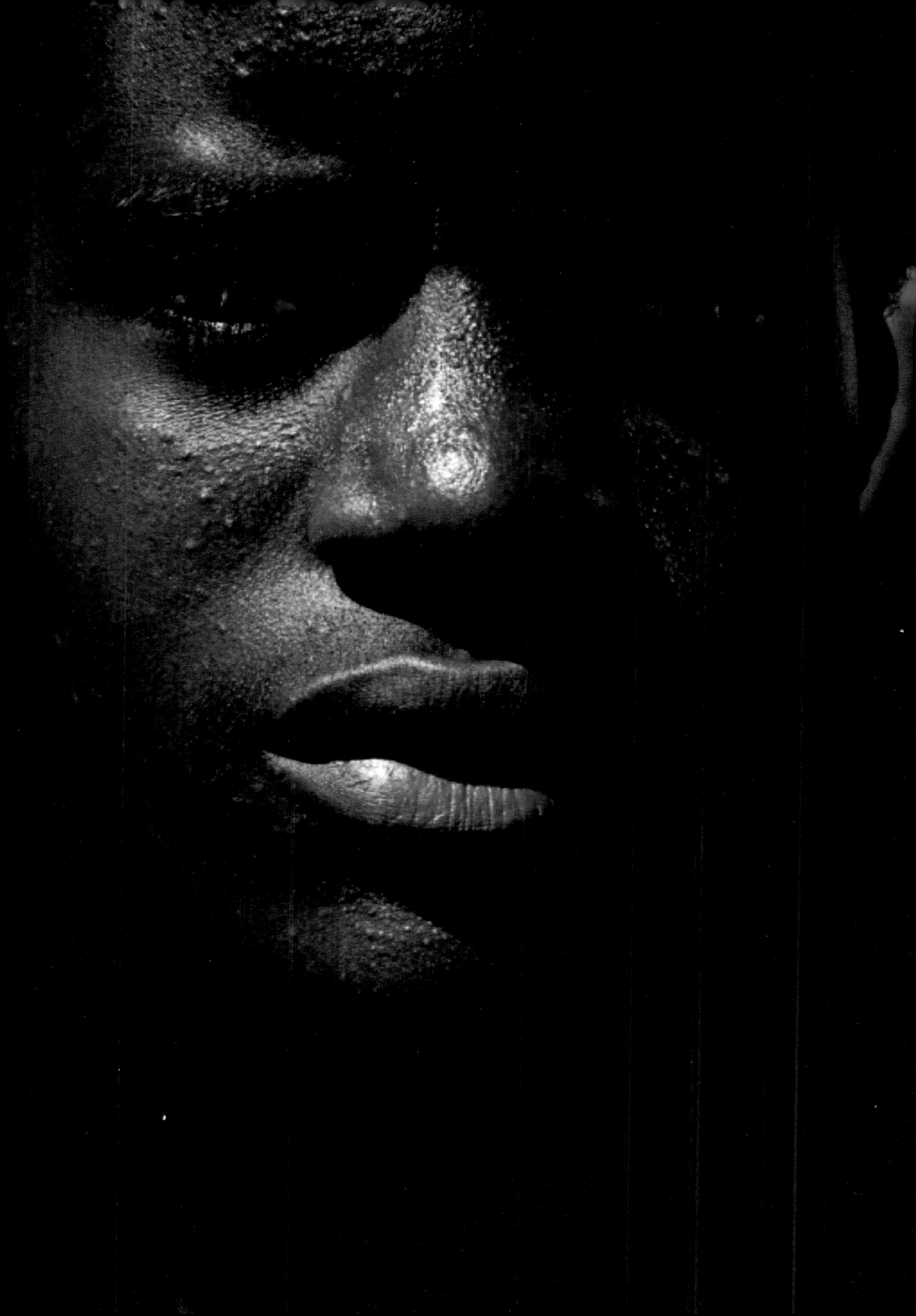

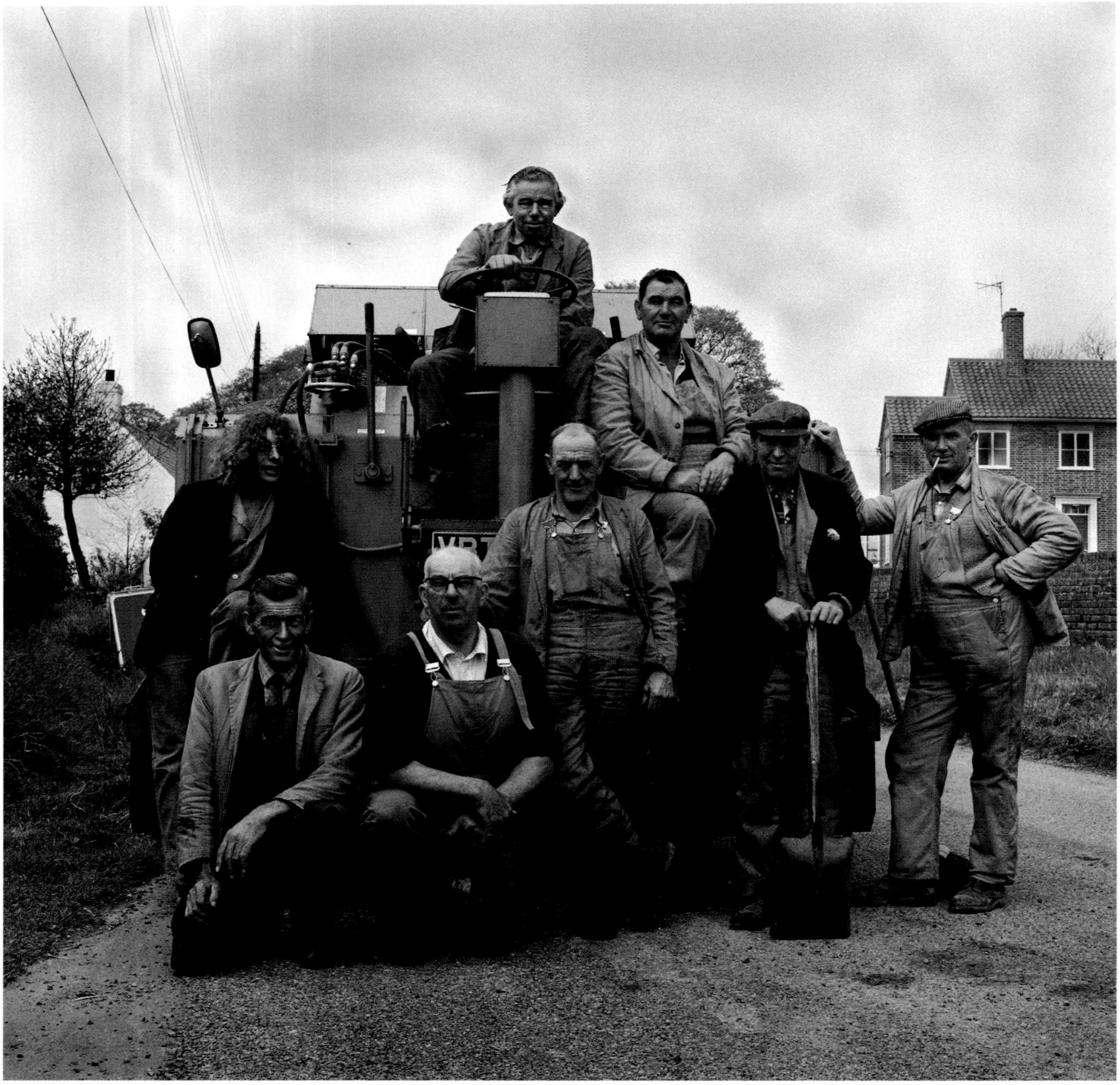

28. Road workers, Yorkshire. 1972

All the time I photographed people's faces
as a guide to their interior lives.
I studied the uncompromising images of Richard Avedon.

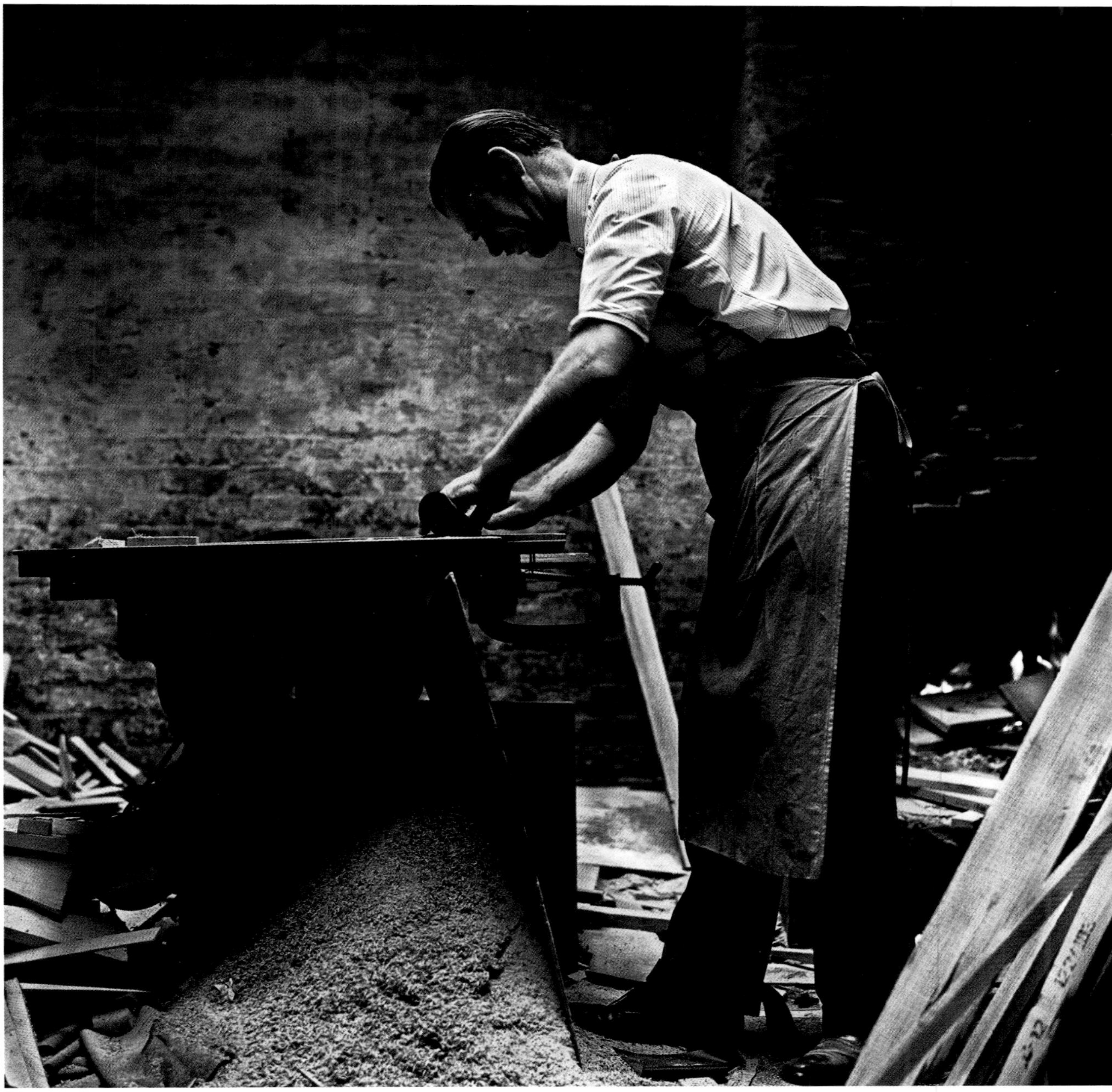

29. Furniture maker, Wapping, London. Summer 1971

I studied the humane images of Irving Penn
and the "one-world, one-people" photographs of Paul Strand.
The intelligence of these images is a beacon to me.

THE PRESS

OBJECTIVE

Freedom of the press is a necessity for a healthy democracy, as is the freedom of the trade unions to organize and defend workers' rights. In the 1970s, newspapers tended to be owned by local publishers whose political views, with rare exceptions, dominated their papers. There was a clear hierarchy which controlled what the editors and reporters could publish. This, of course, meant that then as now truth was a subjective matter to be manipulated or translated at the will of the publisher. Since then there have risen powerful trans-national media corporations which own television and radio networks, newspapers, film studios and distributors, music labels and now internet services. They have come to dominate and homogenise culture, and serve the interests of globalisers rather than local people and local interests. Remember that the word "media" comes from the word "mediate" – which means to transfer something from one place to another. In this "between" state, many changes may occur. Now as then, it is in the interest of the publisher to maintain a culture in his/her newspaper which suits major advertisers. Since, for instance, it is rare that a housewife or textile worker will take out a lucrative advertisement, and more usual that a detergent manufacturer or mill owner will, the inherent bias is almost always in favour of big business rather than the consumer or worker. Truth has a price.

SUBJECTIVE

While I was photographing at a newspaper in the West Country, there was a firemen's strike. One day there was a fire at a house and a striking fireman risked his life to save a child. The young reporter I was with wrote up the story in a positive light and submitted it. He was told by his news editor that it was not well written and would not be used. When he asked why, he was told that as the newspaper's owner was against the firemen's strike. A sympathetic human interest story involving a brave fireman really was not to the benefit of the publisher. The reporter told me that if he insisted he would never get promoted. At best he would end up a sub-editor or be forced, out of frustration, to quit. This was indirect political manipulation of the reporter's attitudes and a way to be certain that only people with attitudes consistent with those of the publisher would be promoted.

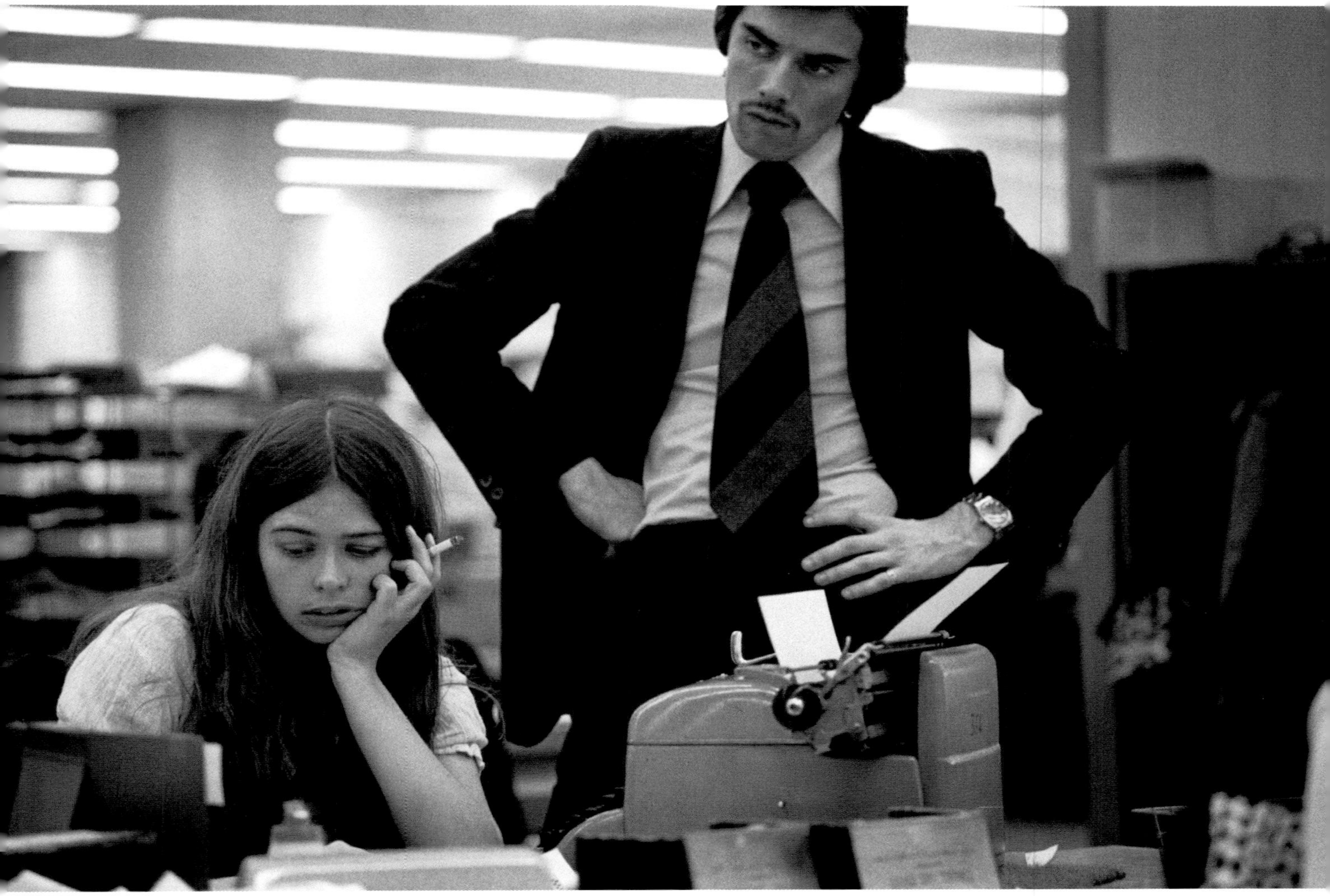

30. Manager and worker, newspaper office, Bristol. September 1976

In Lebanon and Africa, slaughter; elsewhere dictators rose and fell; Reagan's Star Wars plotted mass destruction; headlines were dominated by famines, drug abuse, AIDS and crime.

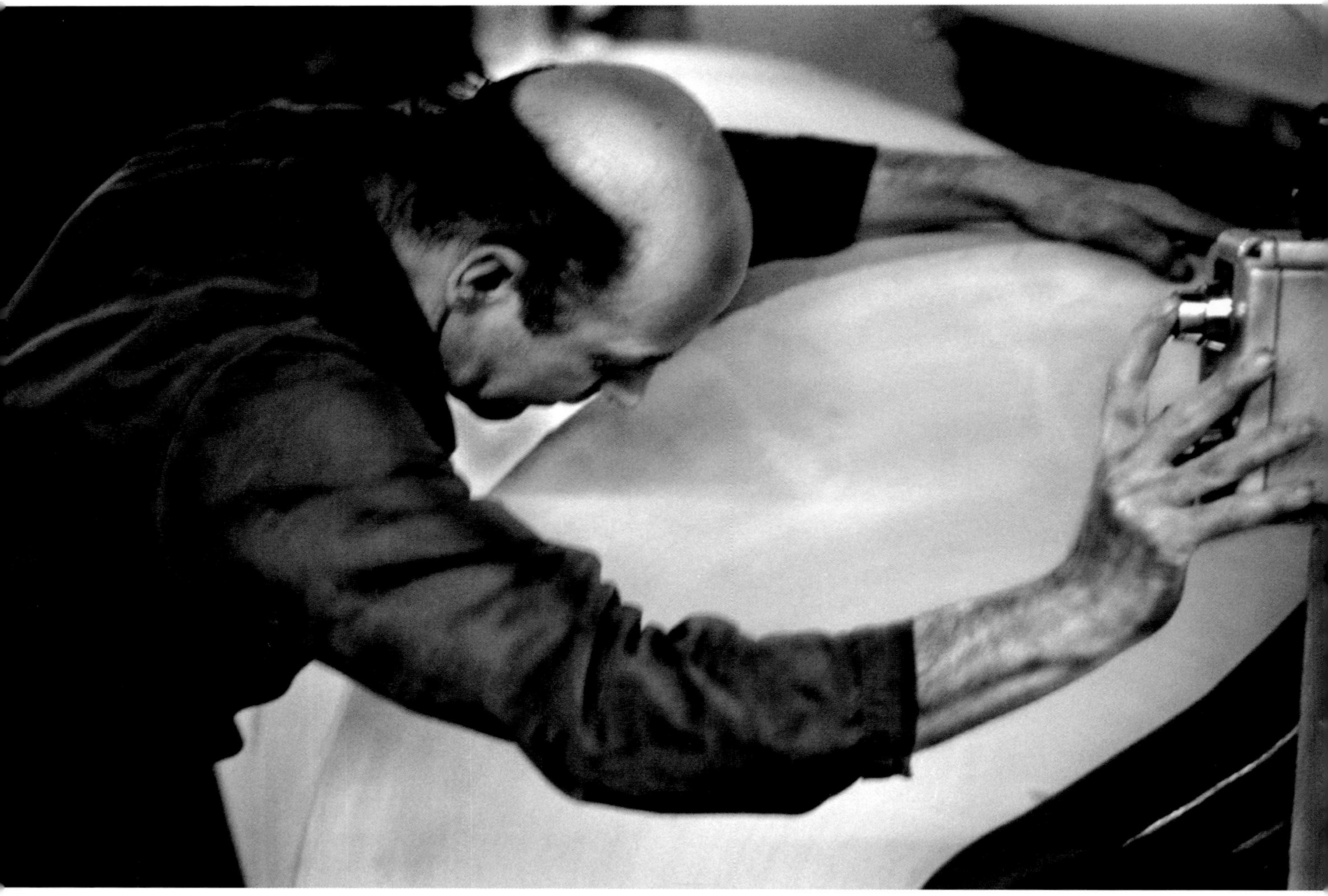

31. Print worker starts the machines, newspaper plant, Bristol. September 1976

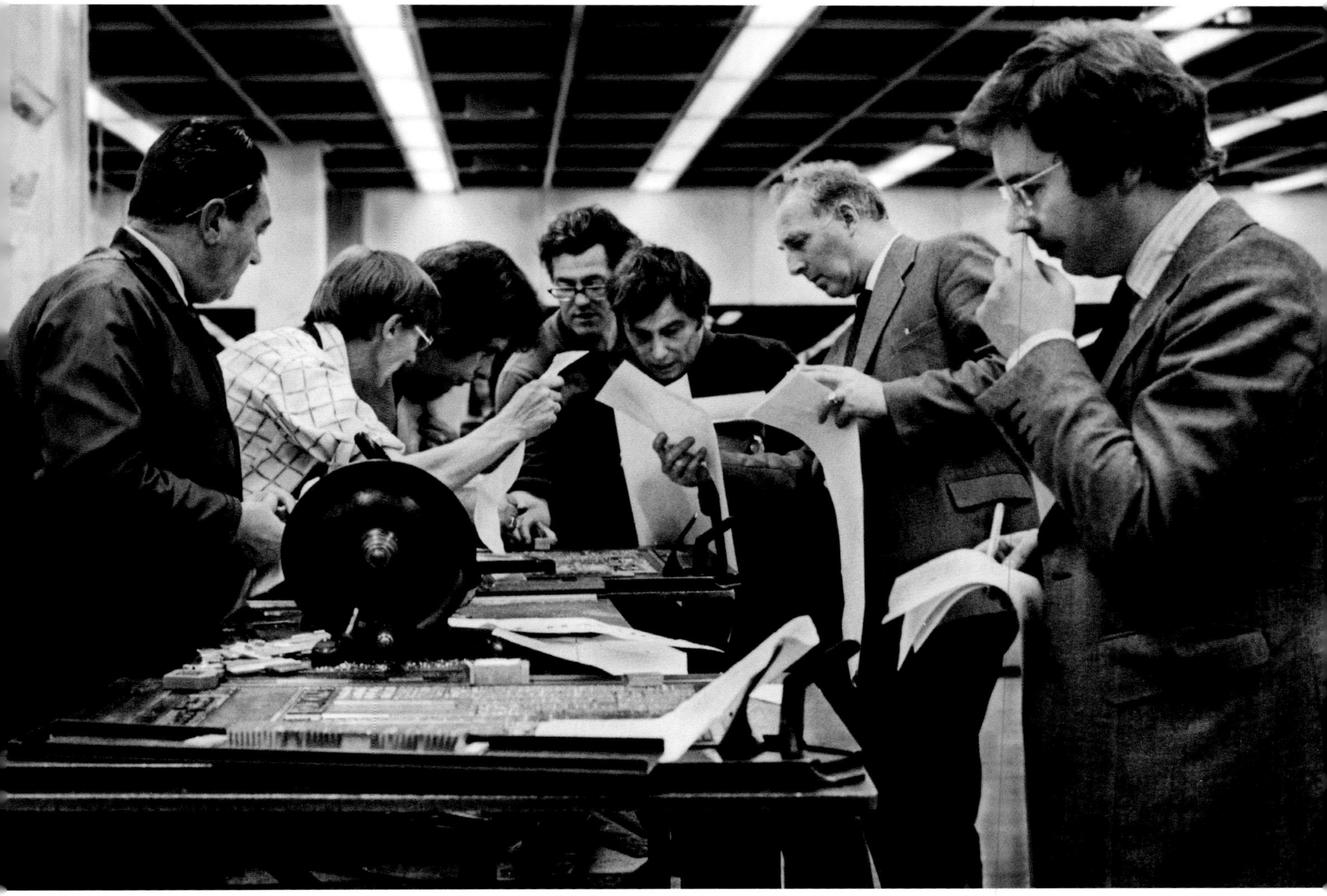

32. Subs and comps (sub-editors and print workers) setting the front page, newspaper office, Bristol. September 1976

My intrusion into others' lives
was an investigation
of their and my humanity:
their intimacy was my own,
their reality was a truth
at one sixtieth of a second
as light gathered behind my lens.

THE SERVICES

OBJECTIVE

In the 1970s, with a failing economy, the public services (schools, healthcare, development and maintenance of the infrastructure) were run down. People lost their jobs, schools and hospitals fell into disrepair, wards were closed, classes grew in size, teachers and nurses struggled to make a living. Britain became characterised as "the sick man of Europe". Strikes occurred as public sector workers became radicalised by falling wages, inability to serve the public properly and by the political atmosphere of the time. Garbage piled up on the streets, firemen were on strike for months, emergency wards became centres of pain and violence, university lectures turned into sit-ins, children shared old text books, libraries were closed. Britain was reverting to the look of the Great Depression of the early 1930s. The very nature of the Welfare State came under assault by the right-wing press. Social Darwinism poked its head up, asking why should those who work hard pay for the rest? Why should we not be more like the United States, where the individual succeeds on merit or accepts the consequences? The fact that bankers, industrialists and the political classes had failed to lead the country towards wealth, to provide the opportunities and education, or to protect Britain's once-dominant industrial position, was ignored, as was the growing influence of global change. The exemplary teacher and the angelic nurse became demonised as troublemakers leading our children astray or refusing to properly care for the sick and aged. It was a time of great social unhappiness.

SUBJECTIVE

Among the hospital workers, I met an extraordinary group of kind human beings who unfailingly showed warmth and tender care to all ages, even when exhausted, which seemed their permanent condition. I remember one ward matron who was tough as old boots and stern with her young nurses, but caring as she dispensed tough love. Her concern for their doing things properly, for their learning how to serve and heal, was beyond question. She told me that she addressed the young doctors by their first names until they became fully qualified – and then had to call them sir, although she said it was understood by all that the matrons often knew more about caring than the doctors when they were still new to the job. One evening, when a child died, she let her guard down and had a moment of painful reflection, her hand held over her face wetted by tears.

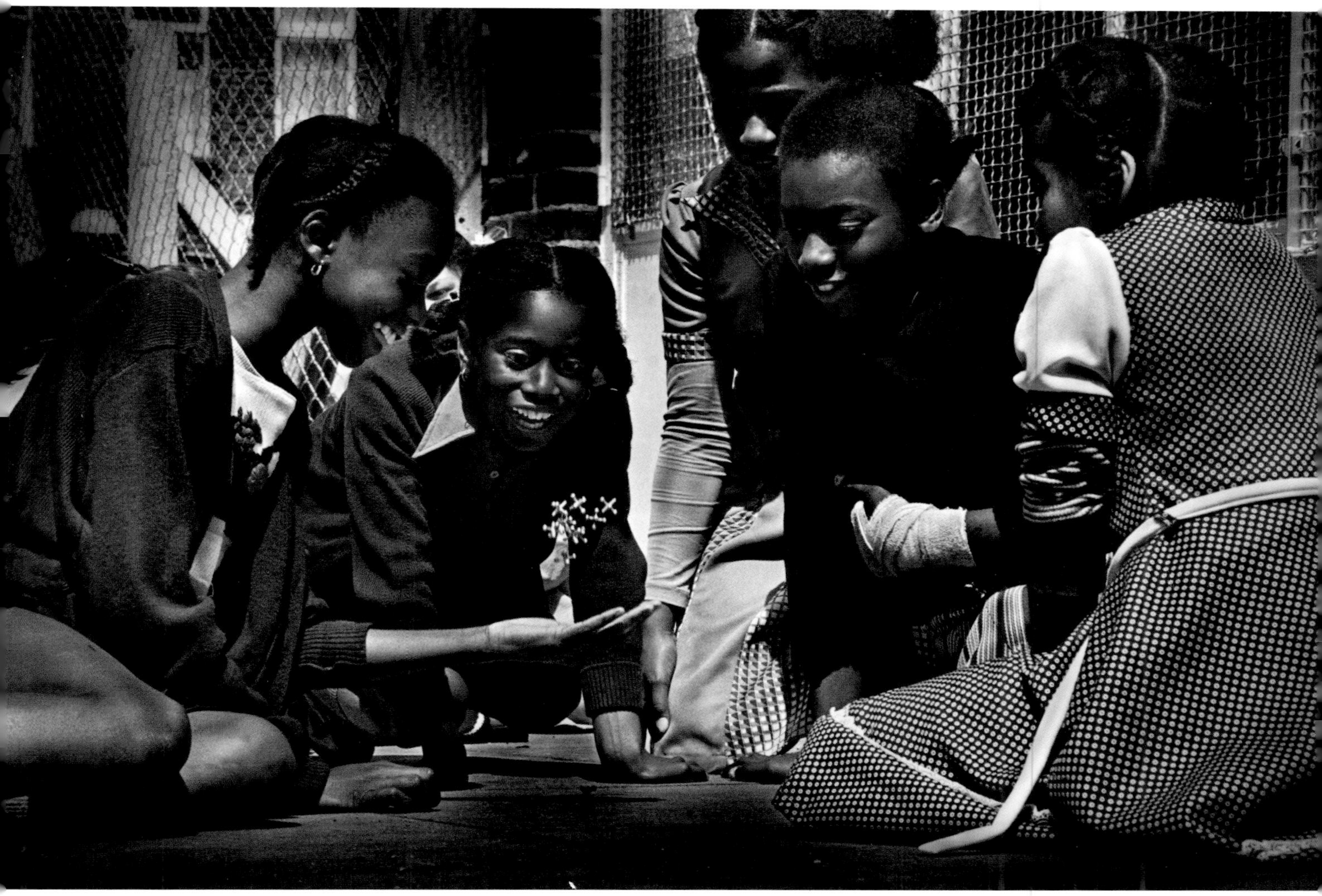

33. Girls play jacks, school playground, Harlesden, London. 1979

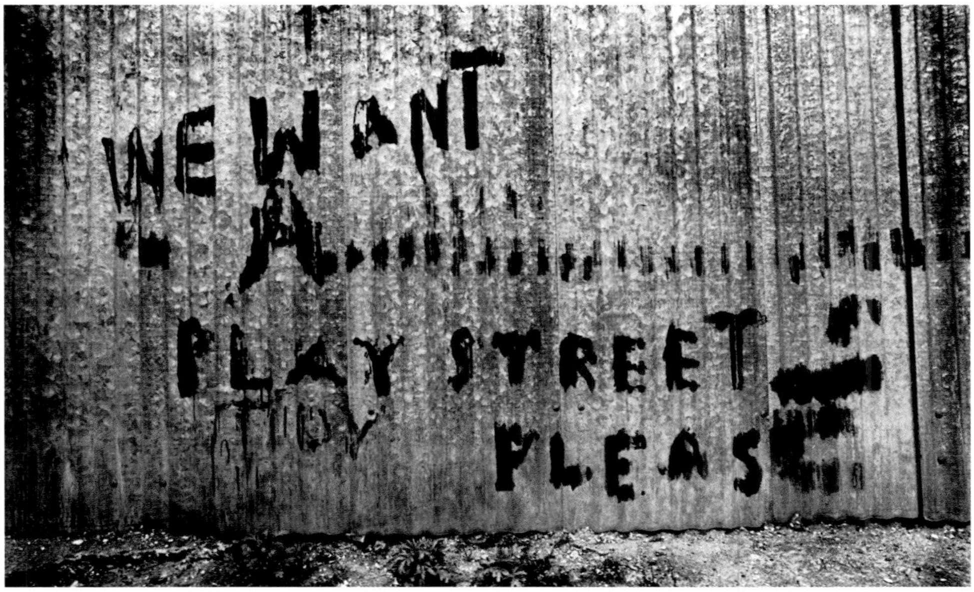

34. Kids street sign, Brixton, London. Late 1970s

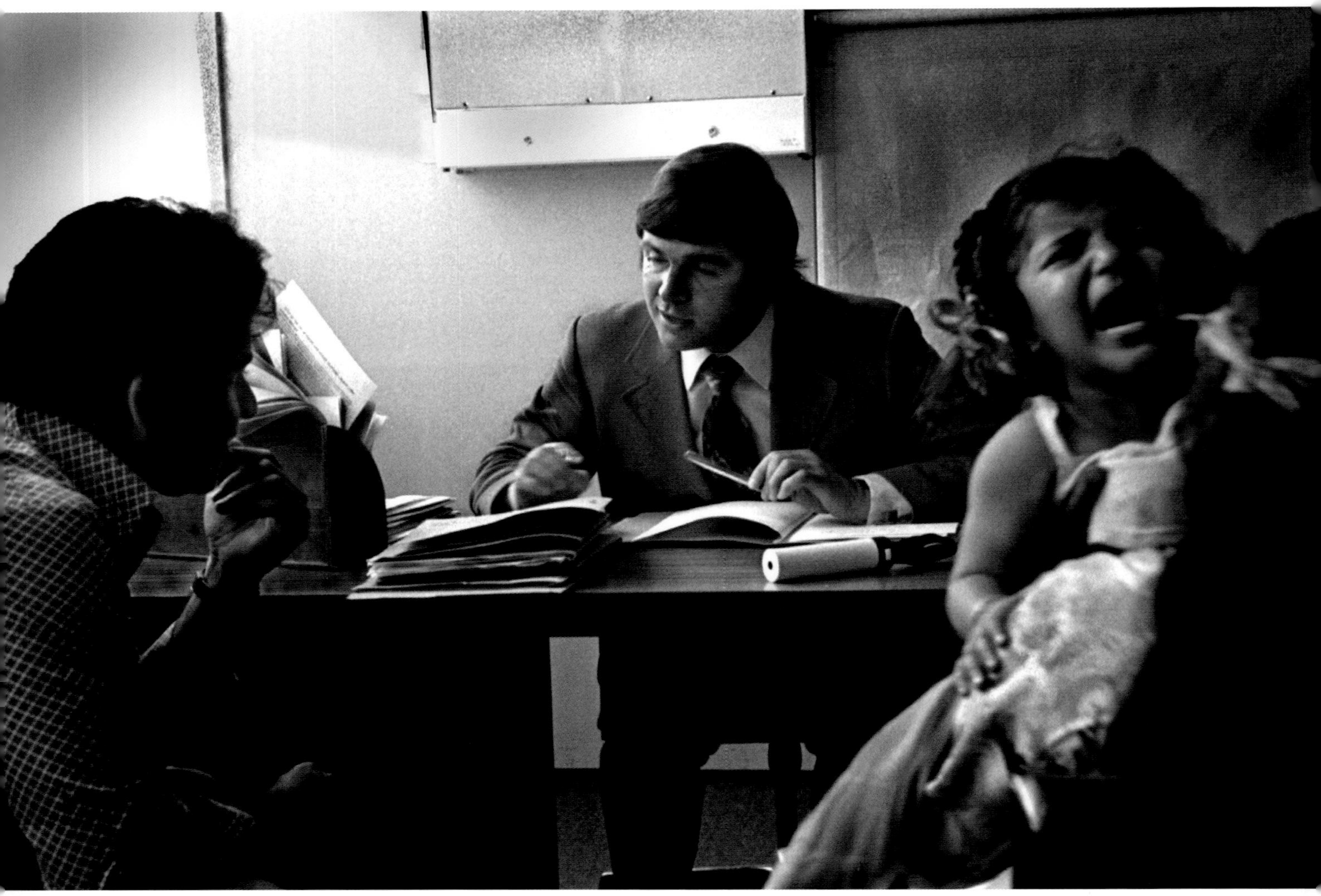

35. Doctor and family, Leicester Royal Infirmary. Spring 1977

I made no claim to the love or possessions of those I photographed
but believed that through my efforts
I was in part an equal owner of their world
as they were of mine.
I was therefore,
at least in my imagination,
a victim, a lover,
a rebel in their lives as they were in mine.

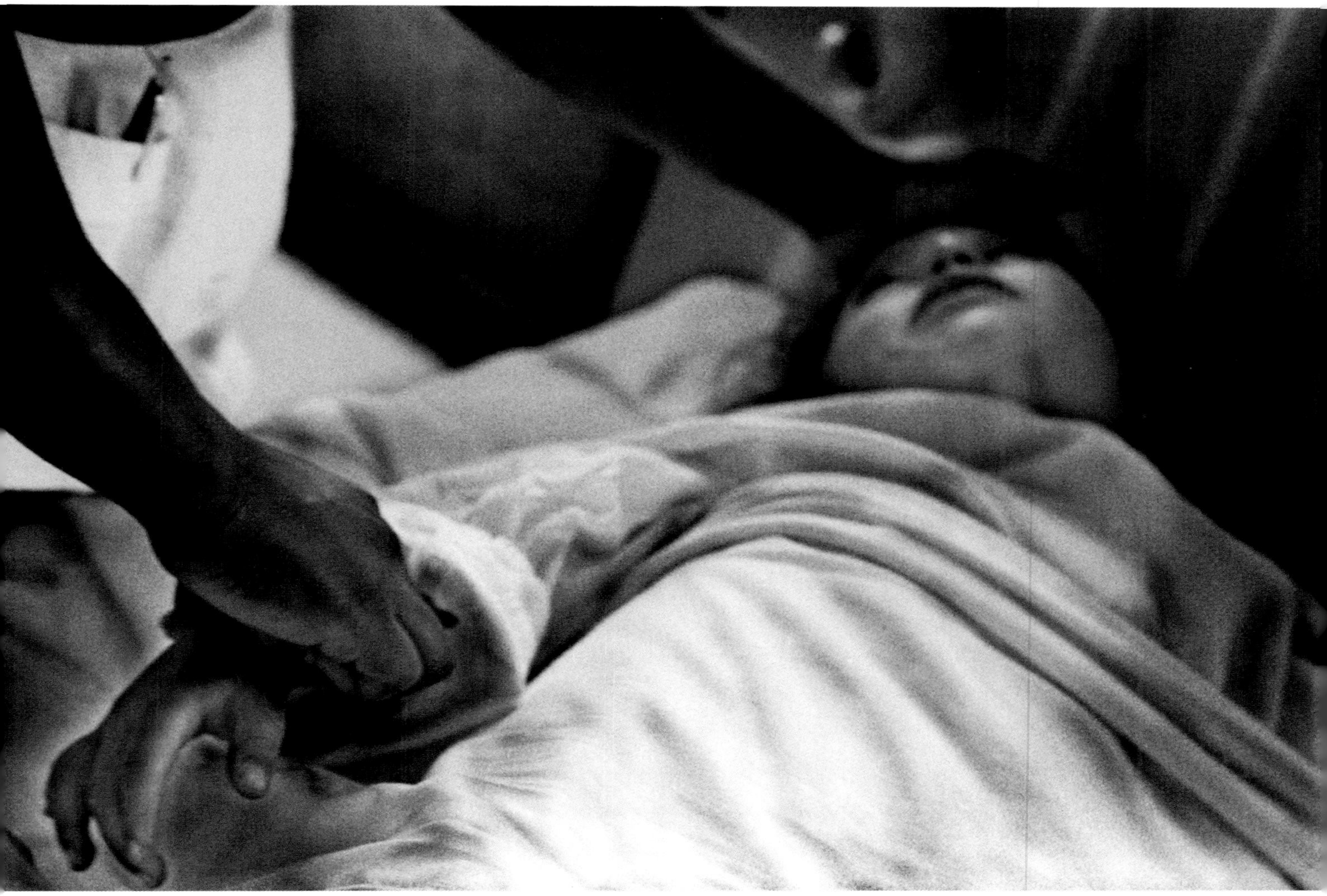

36. Nurse taking pulse, Leicester Royal Infirmary. Spring 1977

I knew that embedded in those circles of confusion were the themes.
Why that – there – then?
I knew all of this was concrete
but that the concrete of class war,
finance, racism, trade and industry
was in itself a projection of others'
compulsion, dreams and madness.

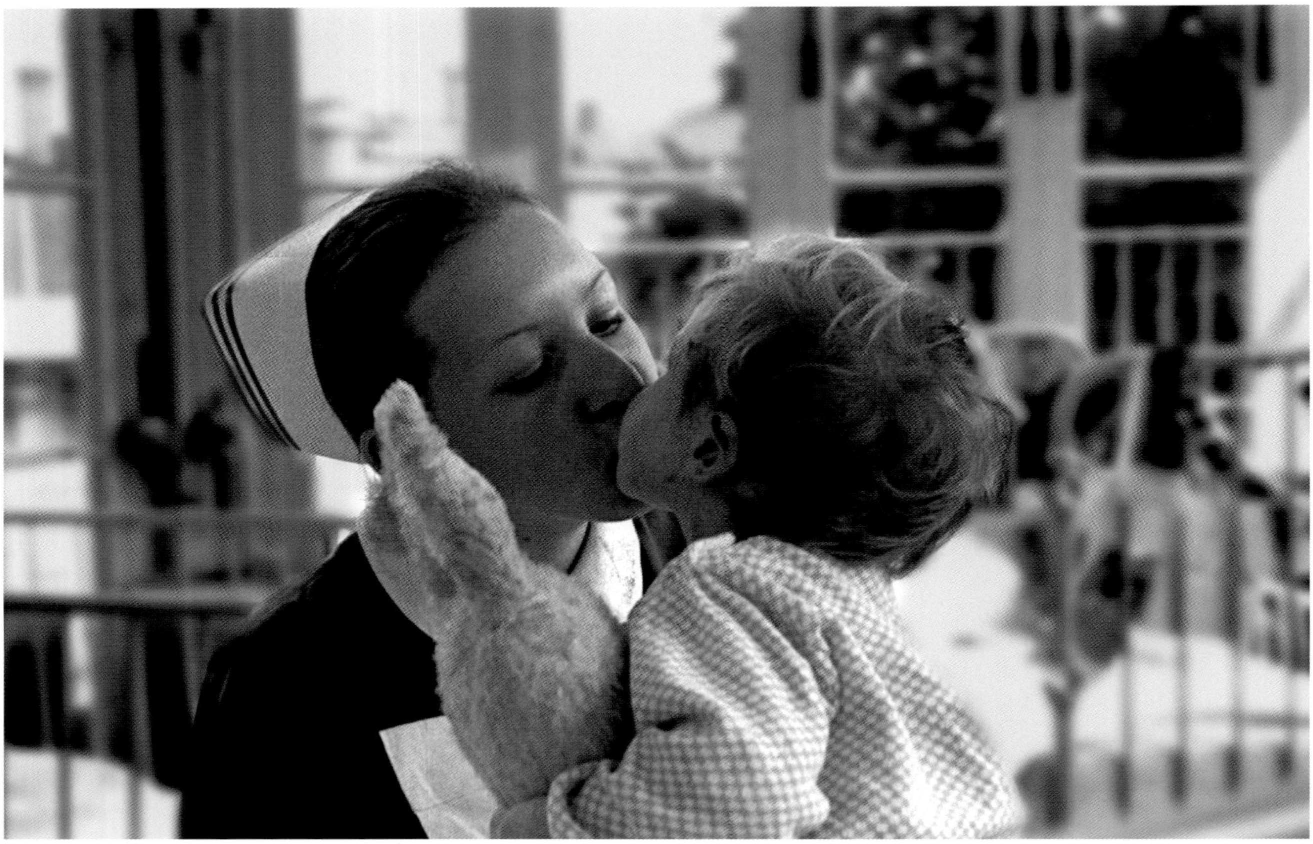

37. A kiss, Children's Ward, Leicester Royal Infirmary. Spring 1977

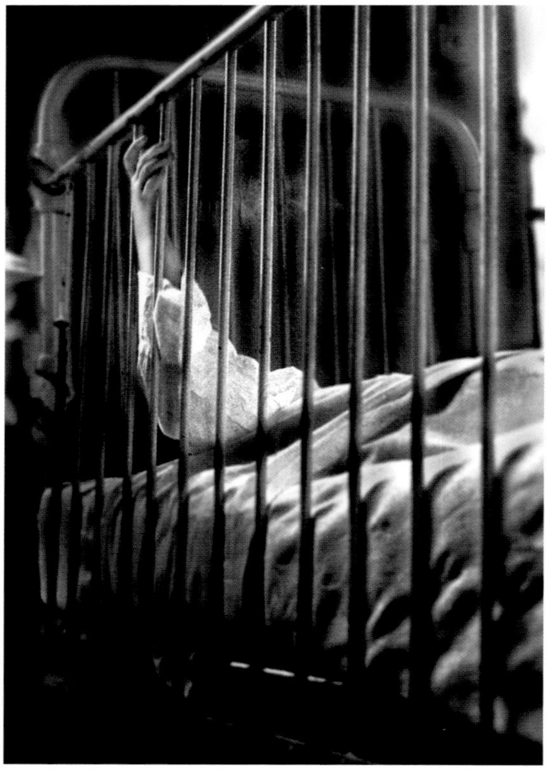

38. Child grasping bed guard, Children's Ward, Leicester Royal Infirmary. Spring 1977

39. Night nurse feeding baby, Children's Ward, Leicester Royal Infirmary. Spring 1977

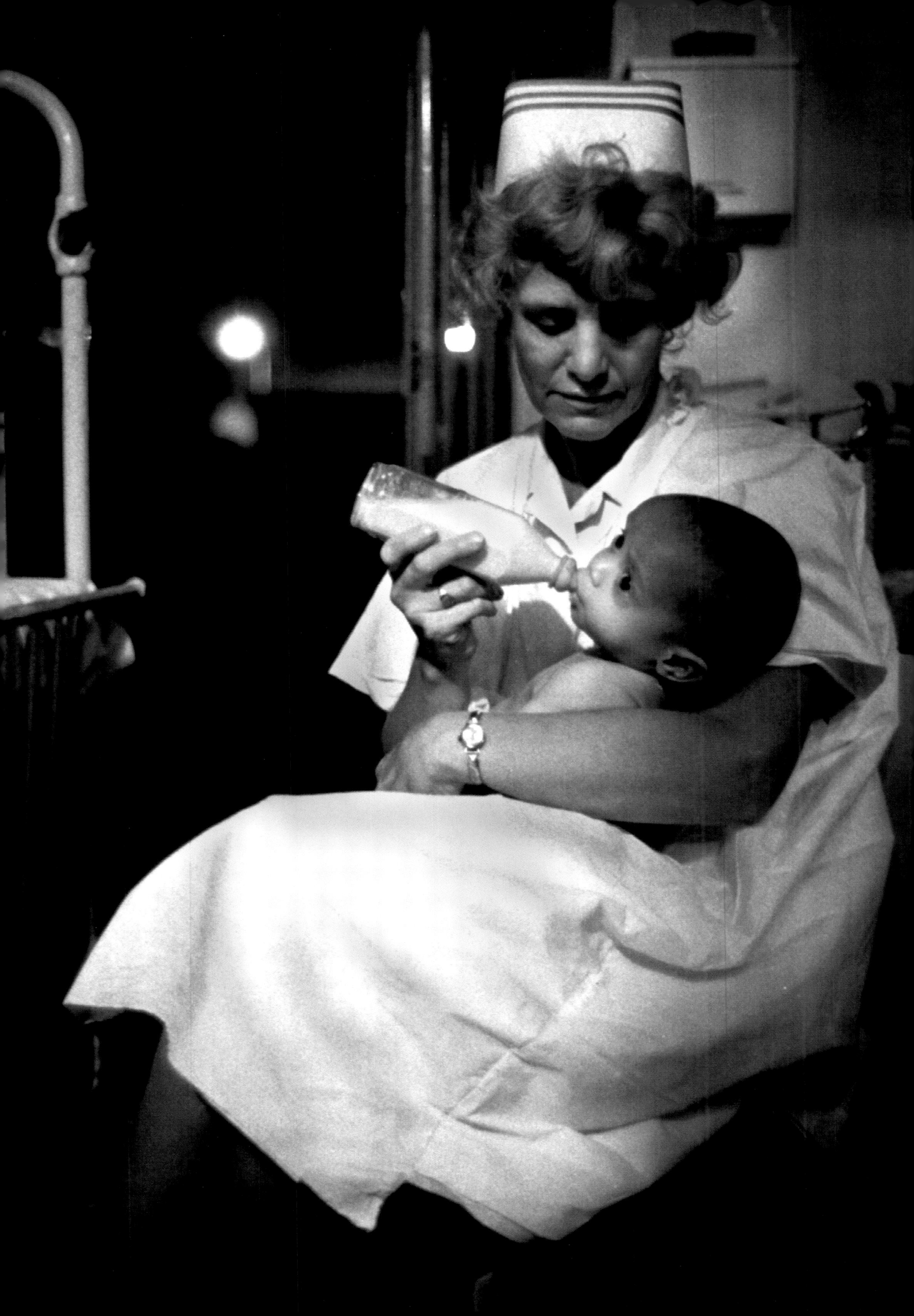

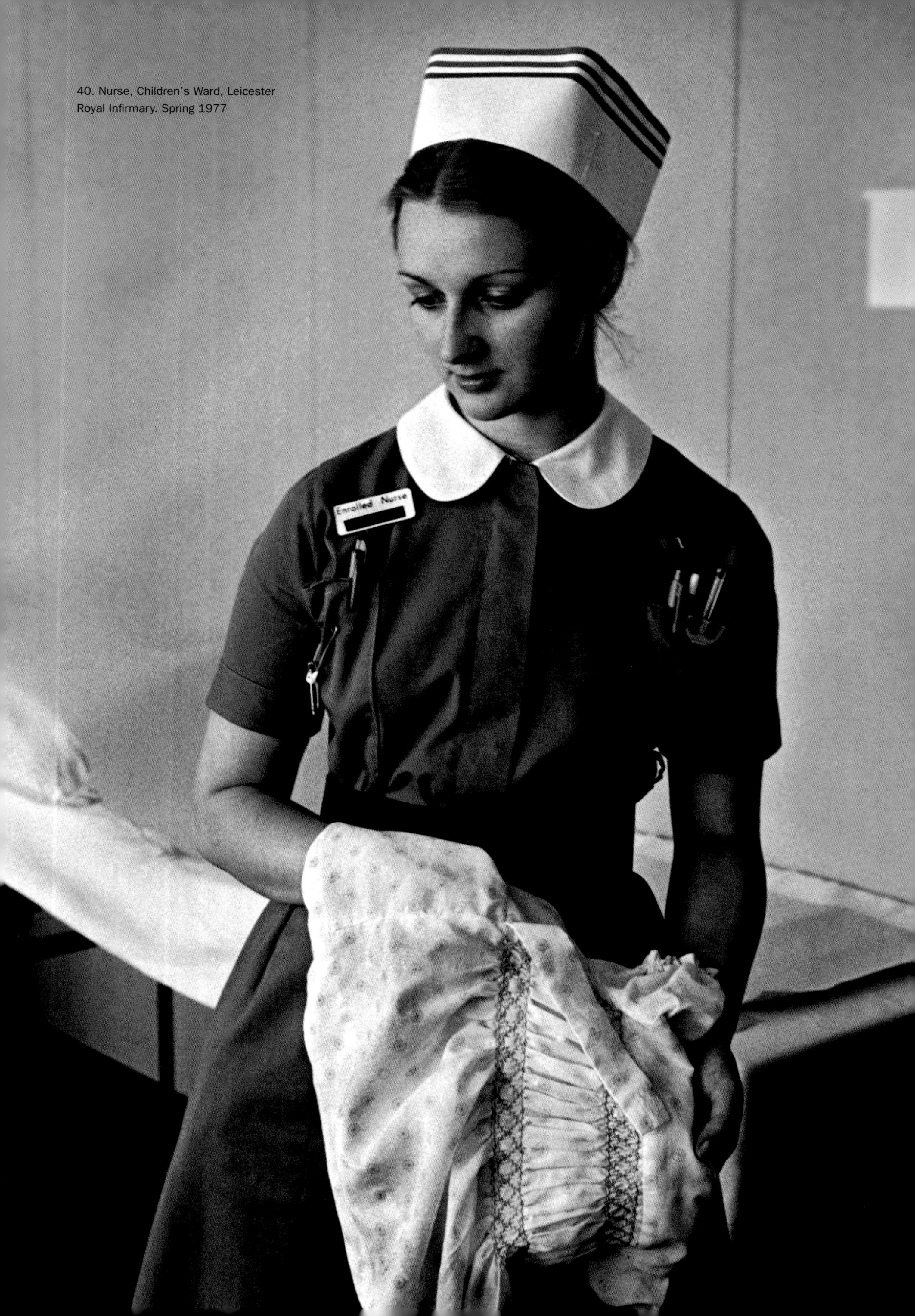

40. Nurse, Children's Ward, Leicester Royal Infirmary. Spring 1977

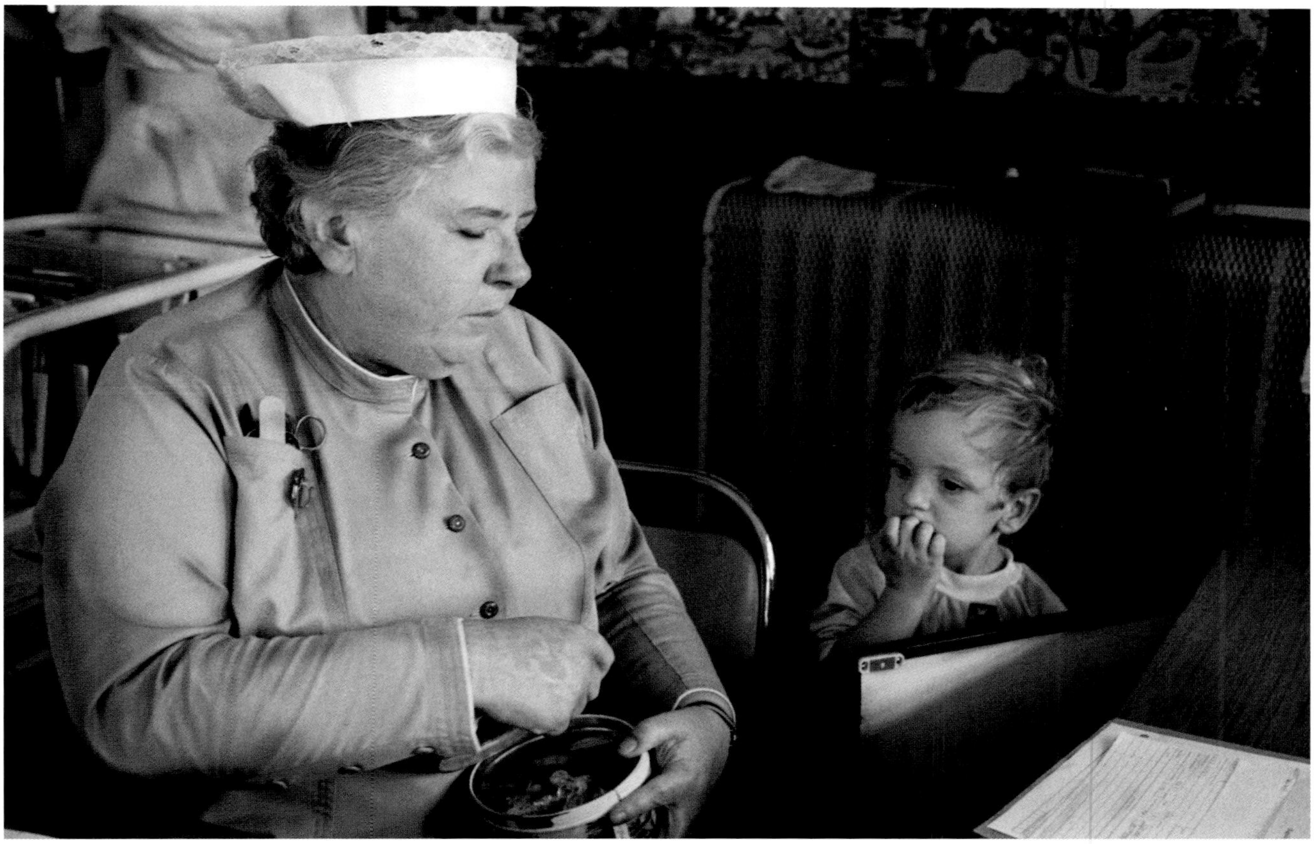

41. Matron, biscuit tin and young patient, Children's Ward, Leicester Royal Infirmary. Spring 1977

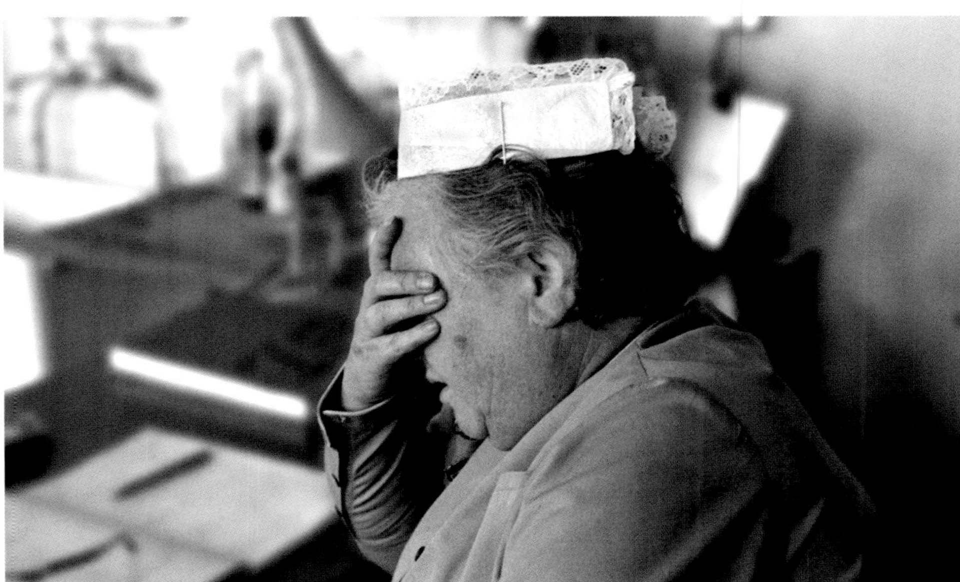

42. Matron after the death of a child, Children's Ward, Leicester Royal Infirmary. Spring 1977

UNEMPLOYMENT

OBJECTIVE:

Unemployment is a pernicious disease that rots the public body from inside. It destroys people's confidence and self-esteem, and leads to depression. Life becomes an endless struggle to survive, to maintain one's stability, to remember love and family. It is a torture imposed by incompetent business and political decision makers on the rest of society. It eats away the fabric of community – families fall apart, neighbourhoods become filthy, houses, shops and public buildings become tawdry and fall into disrepair. At the centre of this is the individual, often blamed by the wealthy and the media as too acquisitive for the wellbeing of the country, too demanding in a period when "we all must tighten our belts." With falling export demand for British goods, increasing competition from modernised European plants and new investment in Third World industry, unemployment in Britain rose to 3.6 million by the end of the 1970s. The welfare state provided a minimum income for families. For two generations, children would learn to live dependent on the state, under-educated and unmotivated to study, develop, work and earn. The community-eye of the traditional working class blinked – and then closed. The apprenticeship tradition of passing on skills in the workplace and membership of the group, the community and the team, disappeared with the closure of the mines and the docks. Young men and women lost their mentors, who were replaced by junk consumerism and an increasingly banal media.

SUBJECTIVE

When I was a very young teenager in dying industrial Detroit, I watched my father pass through a long period of unemployment. I saw him age. I witnessed his excruciating embarrassment when we had to share a sandwich – because he could not afford to buy two. I watched as he argued with my mother over bills and expenses. He glowered and suffered and eventually went completely silent. My mother said he was at least even-tempered – always angry. The politicians called it technological unemployment. I called it a living hell. The faces of the men and women I photographed in Britain in the 70s reminded me of my father's pain. And pain is pain, whatever your gender or skin colour. But the press called the unemployed "scroungers living off the state" and accused hard-working immigrants of stealing jobs and creating unemployment.

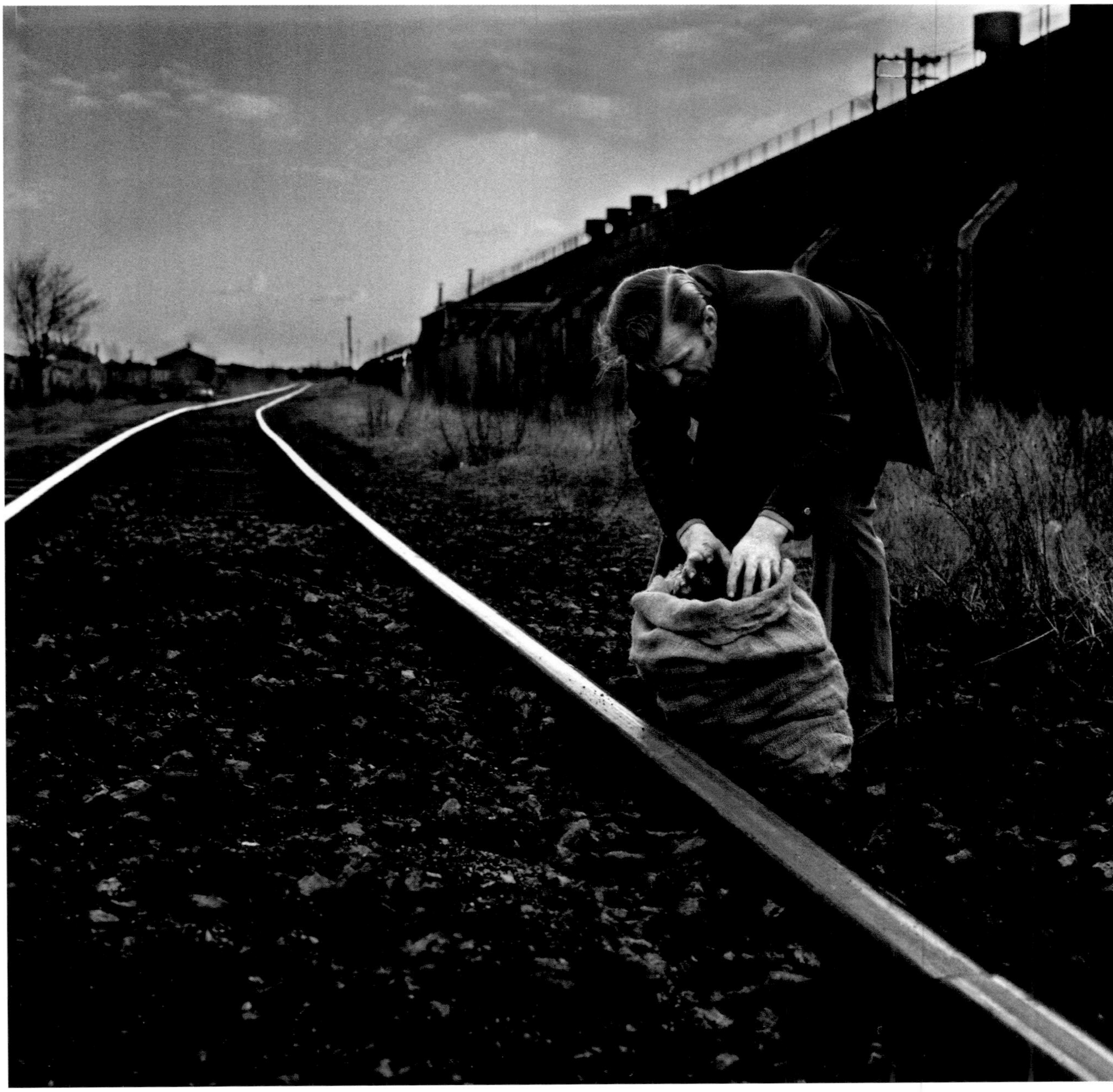

43. Redundant coal miner illegally collecting coal, Tyneside. February 1976

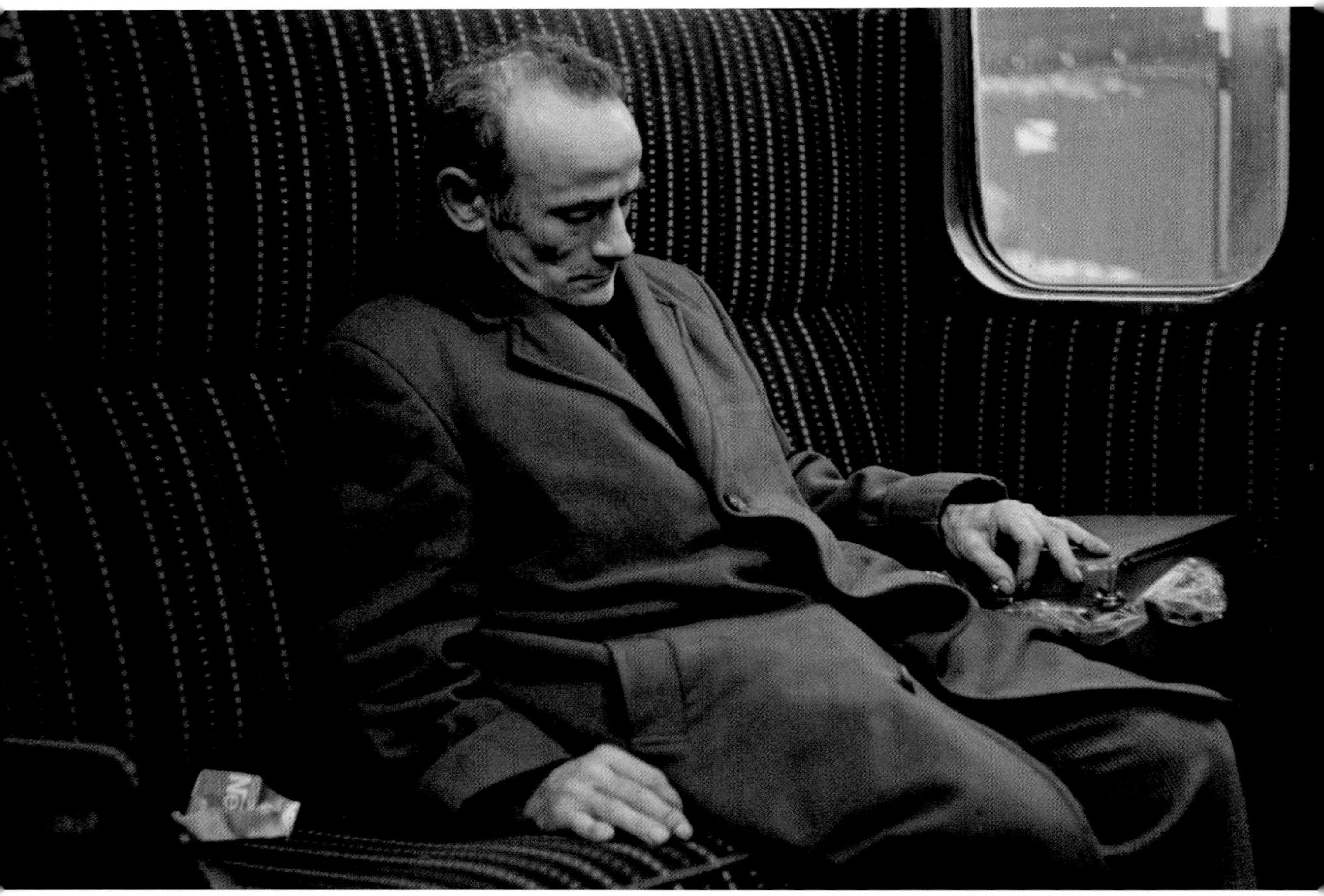

44. Man sleeping on train, West London. Spring 1975

Was my subjective imposition,
this dictatorial control,
different from how anyone else saw a flower,
a building, an exhausted man –
or was it simply unofficial,
somehow subversive?

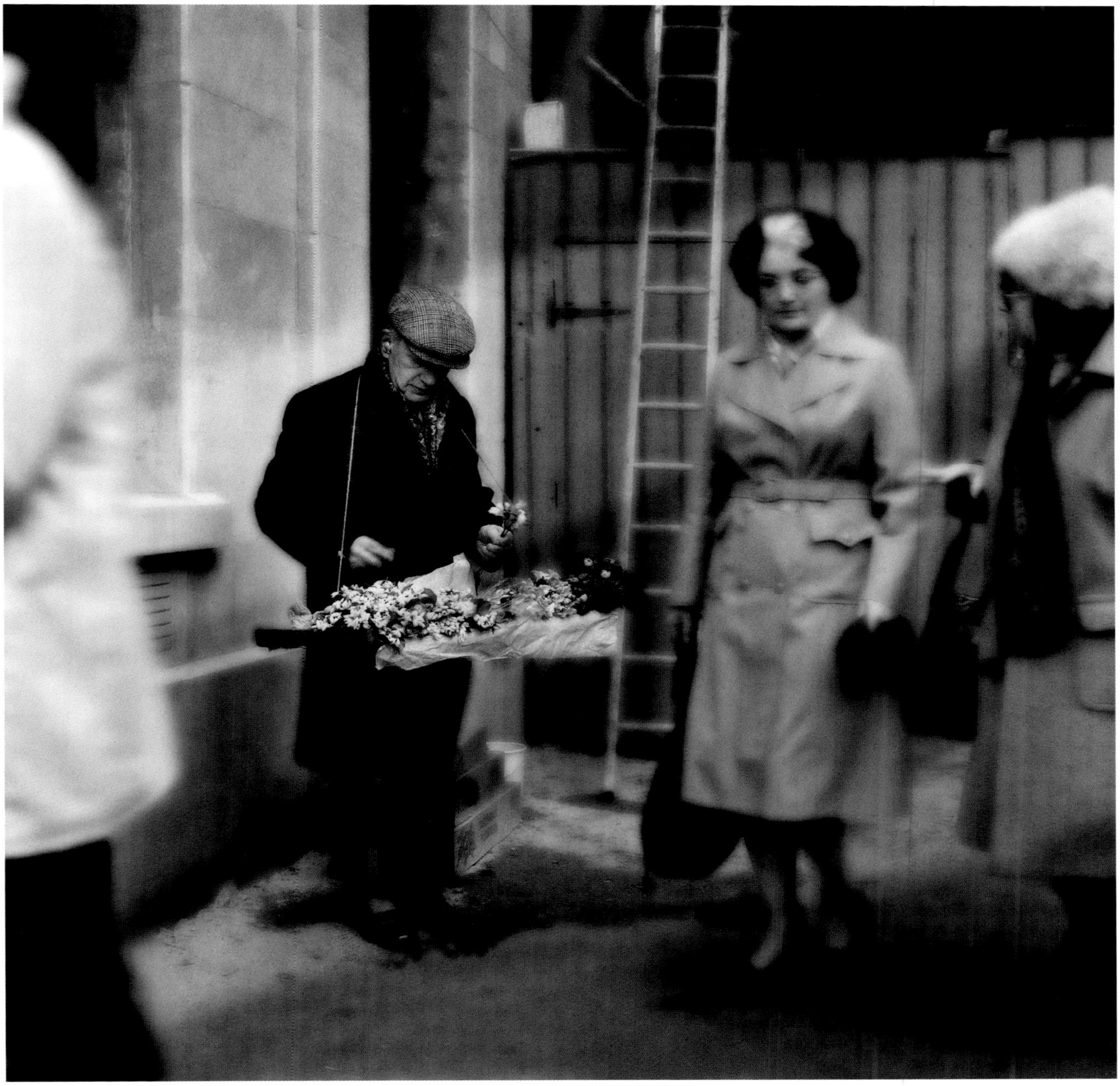

45. Man selling flowers, Tyneside. February 1976

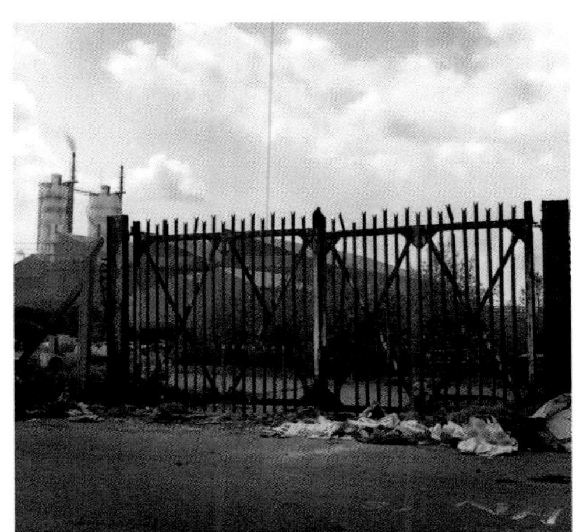

46. Gates, shutdown factory, Liverpool. Spring 1976

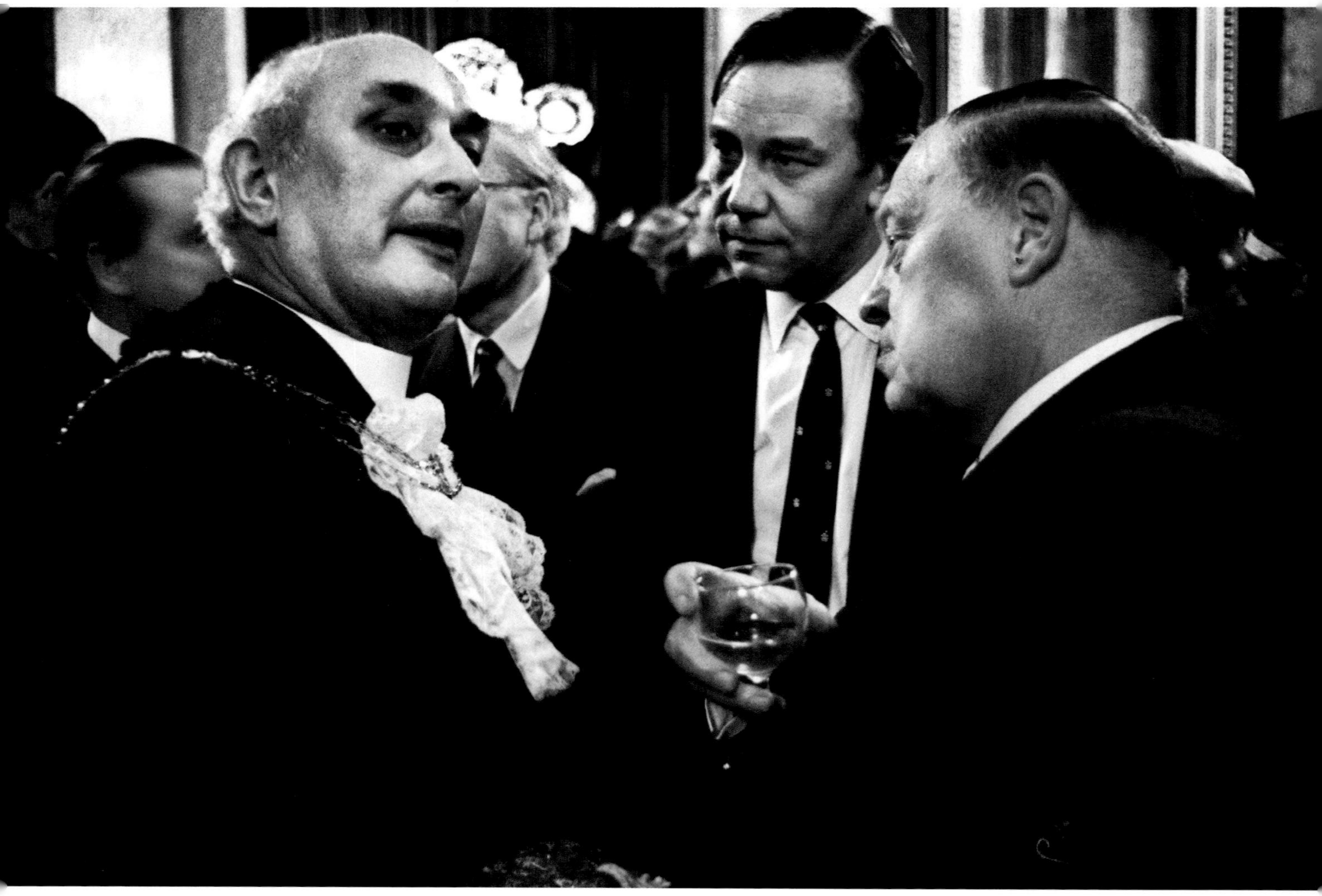

47. Politicians, London. 1972

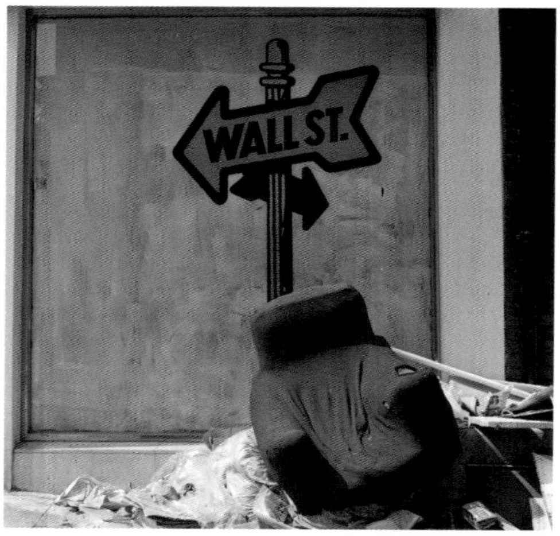

48. Wall Street sign, Hampstead, London. Summer 1976

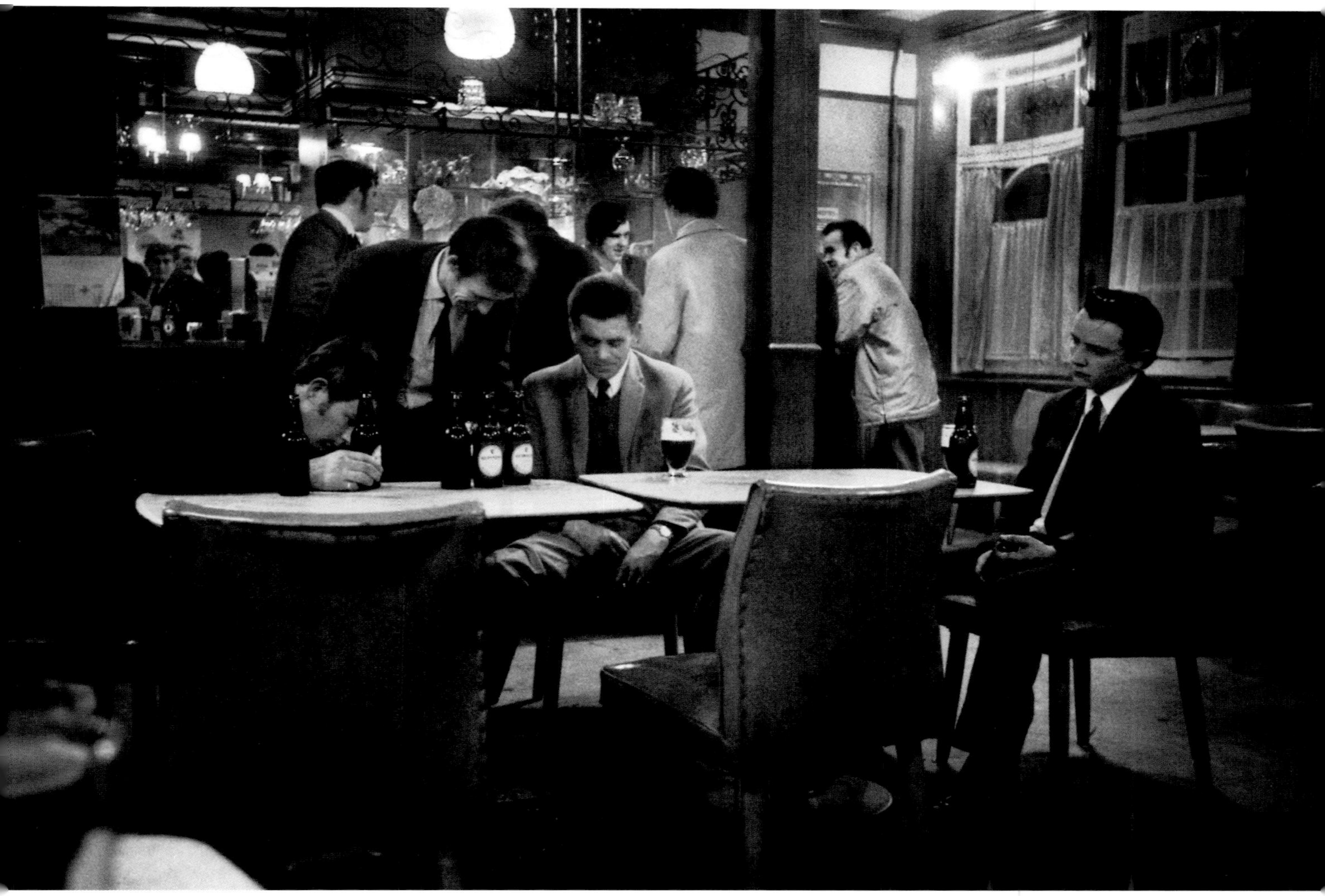

49. End of the day at the pub, Brixton, London. 1977

My precious child would be 28 in the year 2000.
From generation to generation
I wished her to know
what road was behind
so that as she travelled forward,
she would always know from whom and from where she came.

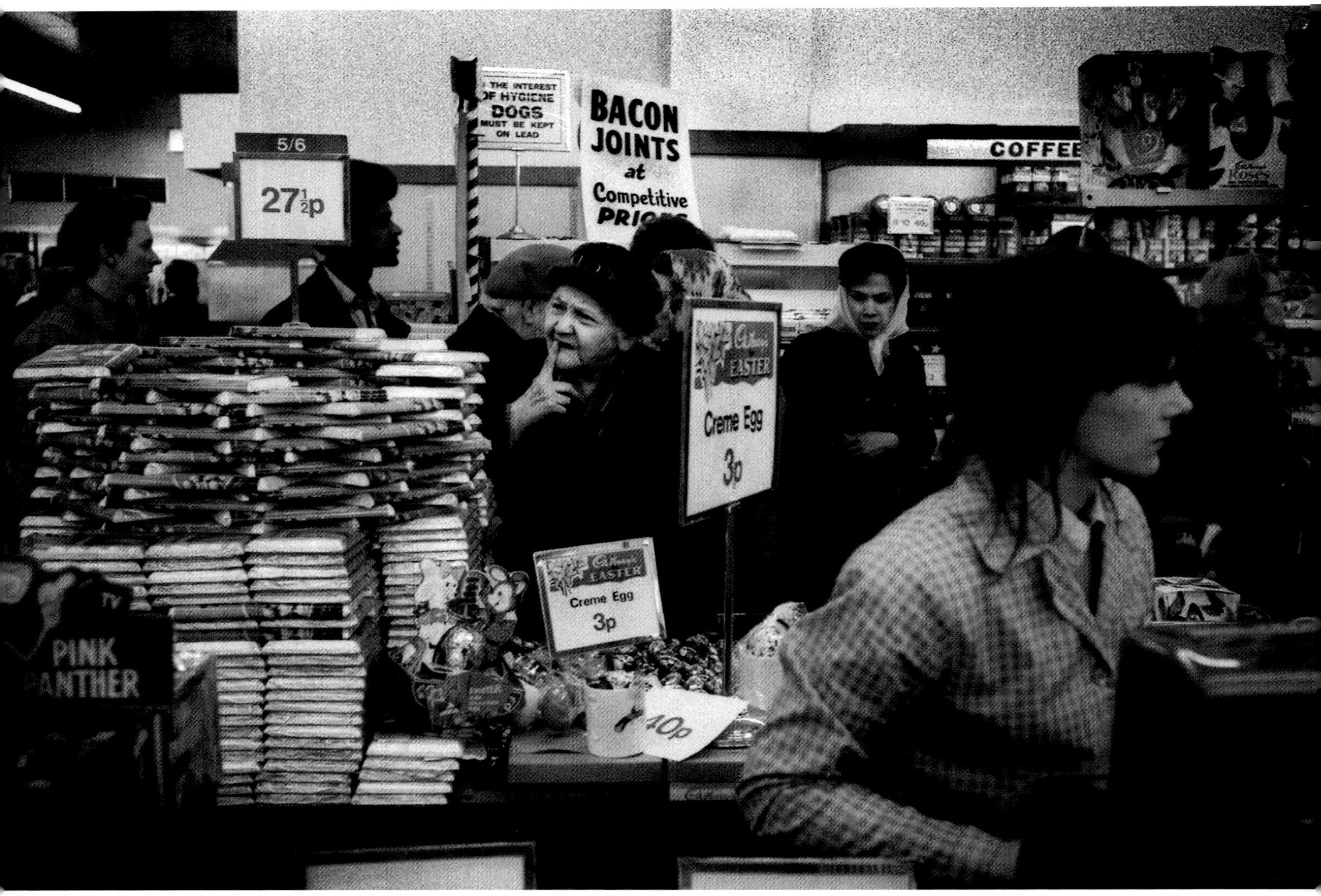

50. Indecisive woman, Woolworths, Brixton, London. Spring 1978

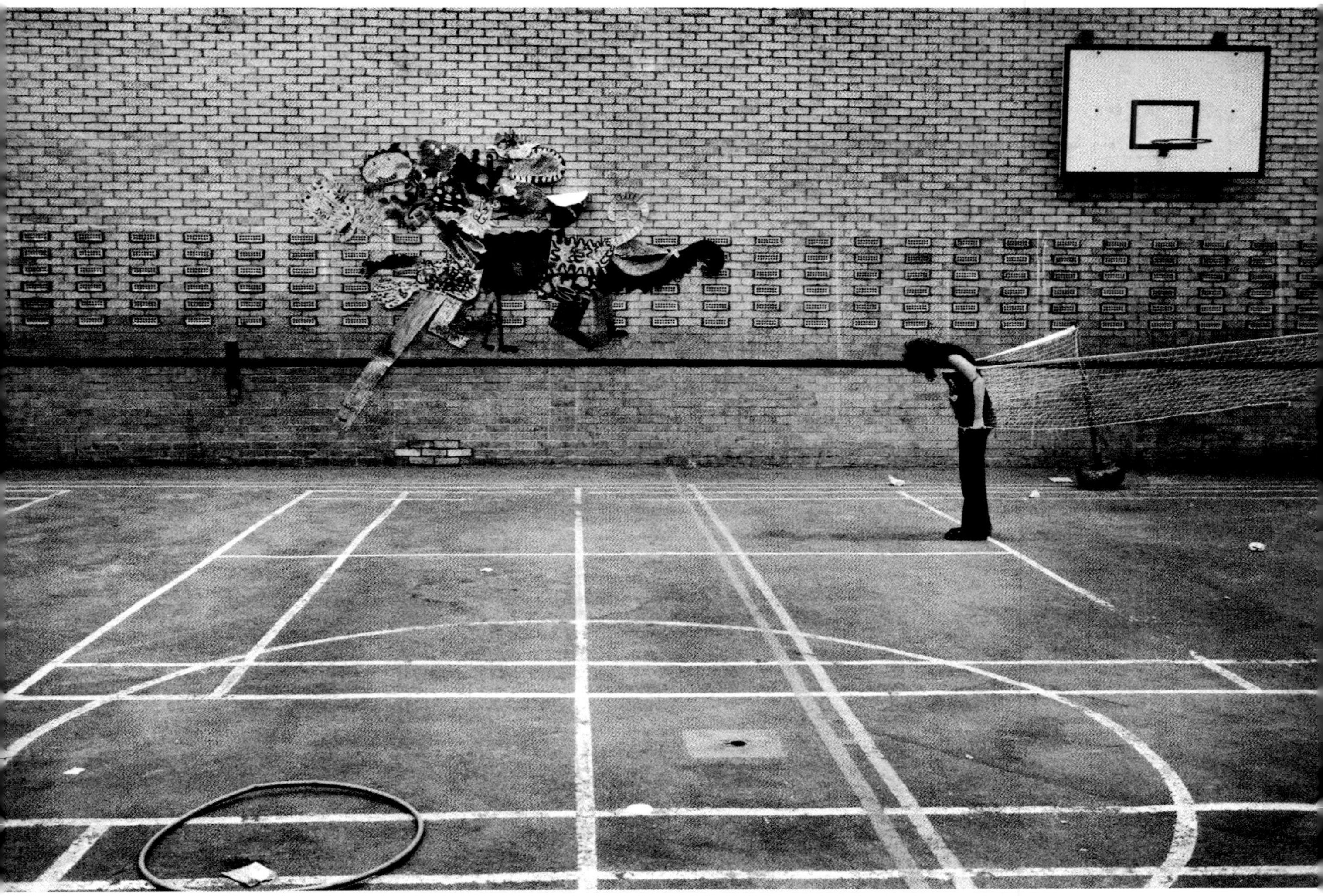

51. Dreaming, gym, East London. 1973

When I was young and struggling to understand, I read
"in the future the flowering of humanity would one day occur
on the concupiscent tip of history's twisted stem"
and that we, my generation,
marching, trashing, chanting, drugging, celebrating,
screwing, sloganeering, fighting, dying and singing
those oh so hopeful sweet folk songs,
that my generation would participate in the blossoming ... but we failed.

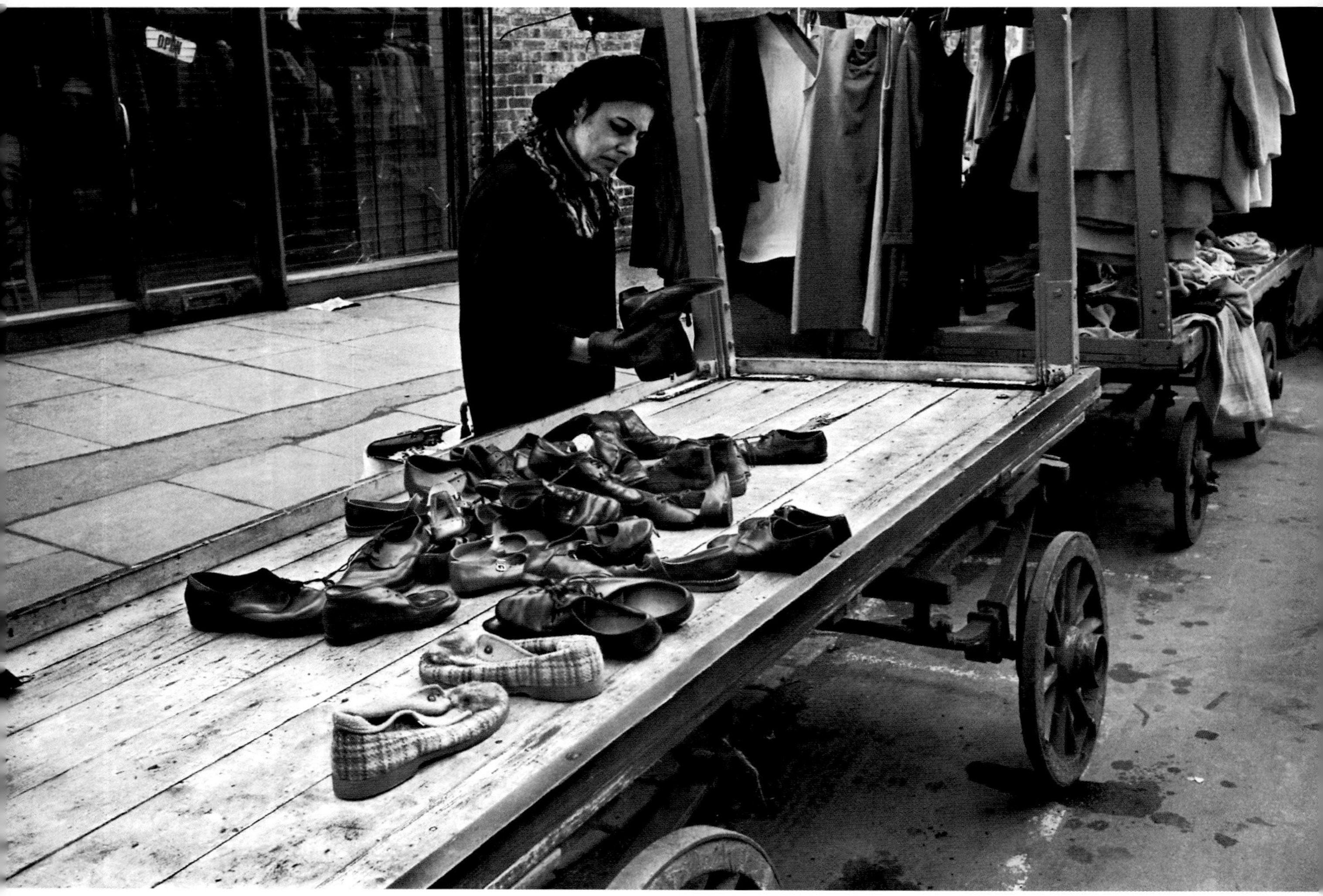

52. Buying shoes, Brixton Market, London. November 1978

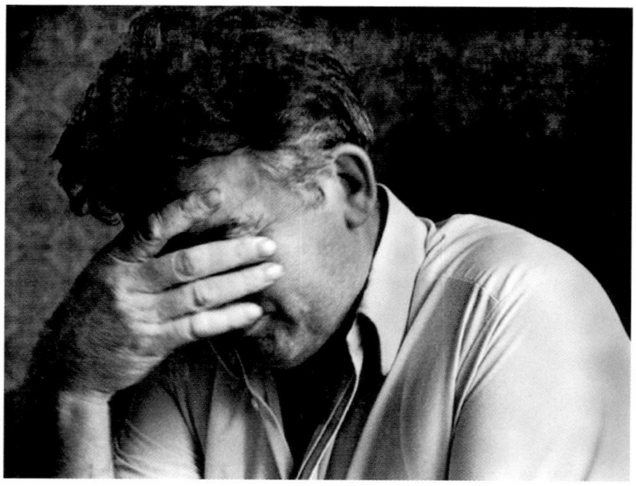

53. Unemployed man, Harlesden, London. 1977

54. Unemployed man during radio interview, North London. 1978

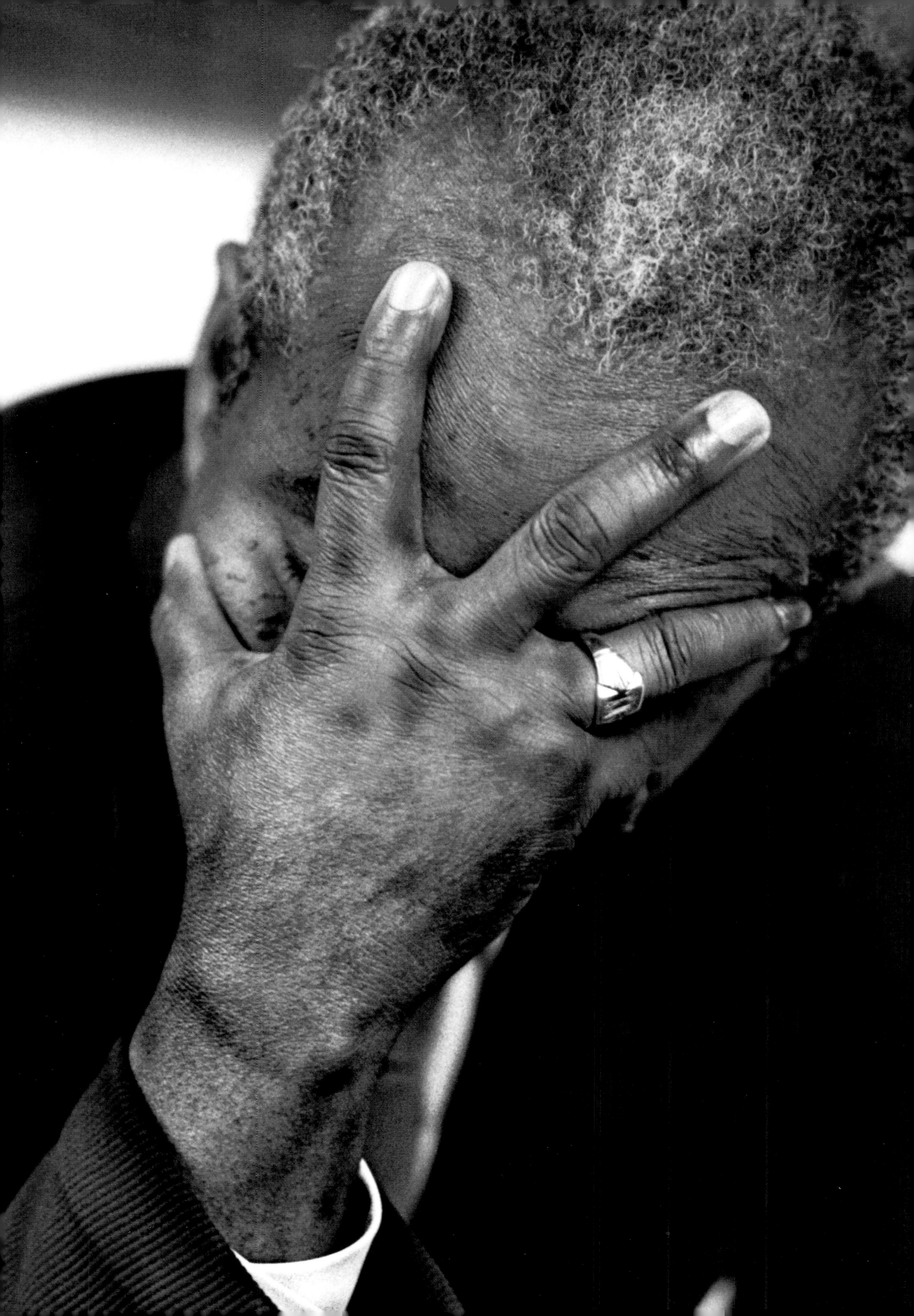

RACISM

OBJECTIVE:

Racism is a defect in the human temperament burned into us by opportunistic political poison. Suspicion of the unknown and of those different from us is, perhaps, not unnatural, but turning this into active hatred and turning that active hatred into action – in particular violent action, is an exercise of political manipulation. The manipulators must foster a plot to frighten the population into believing they are under threat by a force which is sinister and intent on their harm. Your jobs, your daughters, your wellbeing in your house, your peace of mind, your very bodily safety, must be seen to be under attack by The Other – the Moslem, the black man, the Jew, the Protestant, the unemployed, the hoodie, the country hick, the city slicker. And after days or years of hatred, mayhem and death we ask ourselves: "How did this happen? Who told us these people were the enemy? How could we believe they were at fault or meant us harm?" The answers will always be found among the social opportunists, the petty politicians needing a cause to promote themselves, the power and money boys who wish to divide the people, the religious fundamentalists and fanatics who want to impose the One Way on the rest of us. In the 1970s, with rising unemployment, poor education, a muck-raking press and a need to point the finger at someone other than the decision makers, the Afro-West Indian population came under attack, were blamed for displacing British workers and became the butt of political ill will. It was, and still is, a disgrace for a civilized people.

SUBJECTIVE

I had the privilege of being admitted to the West Indian community and quite naturally one personal contact led to another. I found warmth, kindness and, among the older people, a strong religious belief and a determination to work and make their lives better. Unfortunately, the traditions of slavery, which fostered broken homes and fragmented families, were still a cancer in the community, leading to many single-parent families and a sense of disillusionment. Could I photograph a black child one day and the next day a white child, and see a difference in their humanity, in their desire to be happy and to live free of fear? Could I determine that one was more worthy of educational or social advantages? No. The creation of "otherness", of separating ourselves from other people, is alien to me. I am convinced most of us want to be left alone to eat our jam, make our families and live a quiet life.

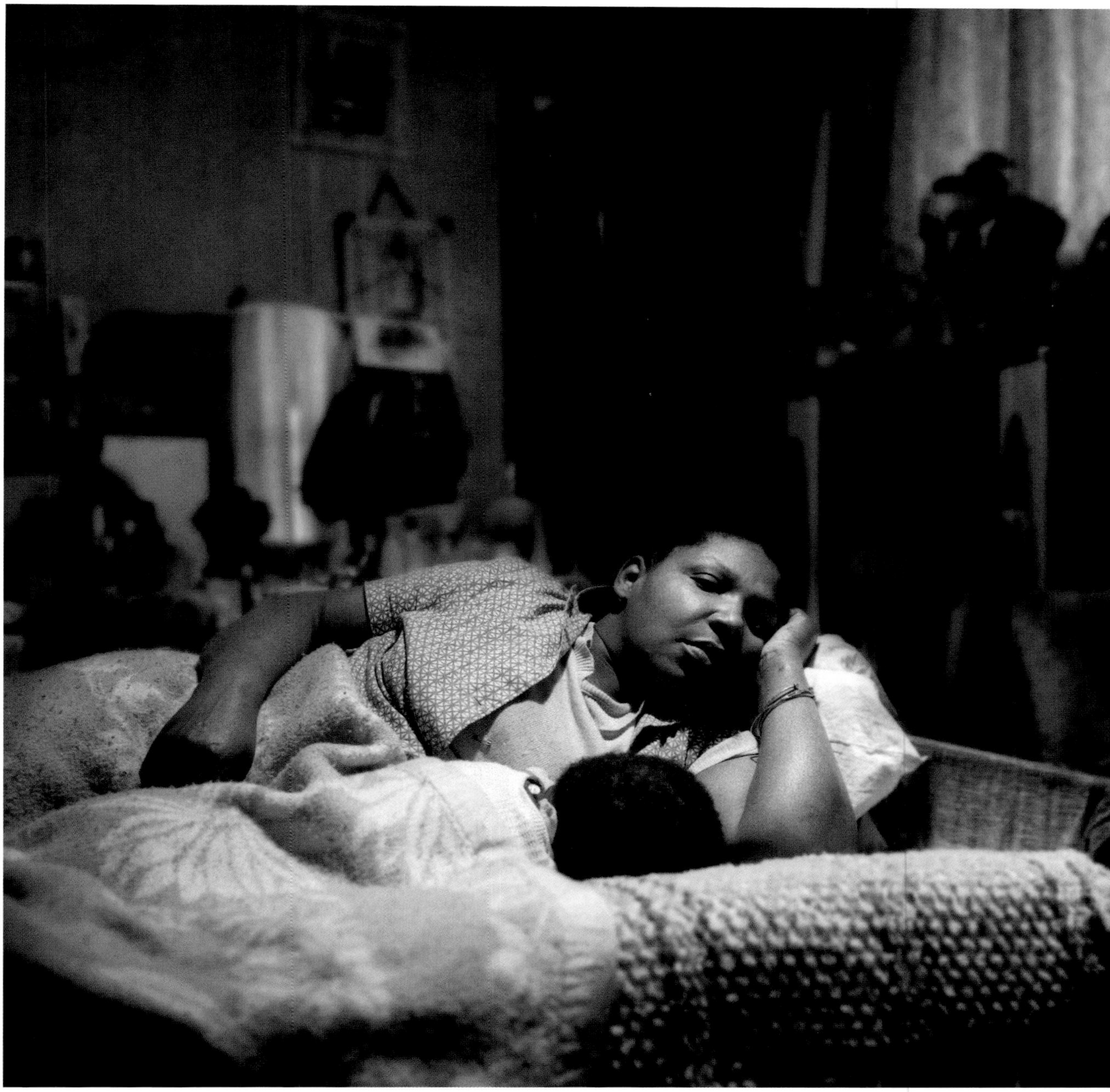

55. Woman and child on bed, Brixton. 1976

I had dreamt that I, a photographer, would reveal truth.
Truth would expose injury.
Injury would be healed by the encyclopaedia of justice.
But the encyclopaedia became a Bible:
rules to kneel down to,
the Bible became a storybook of life:
a beginning in love
a middle in dreams
an end in sorrow.

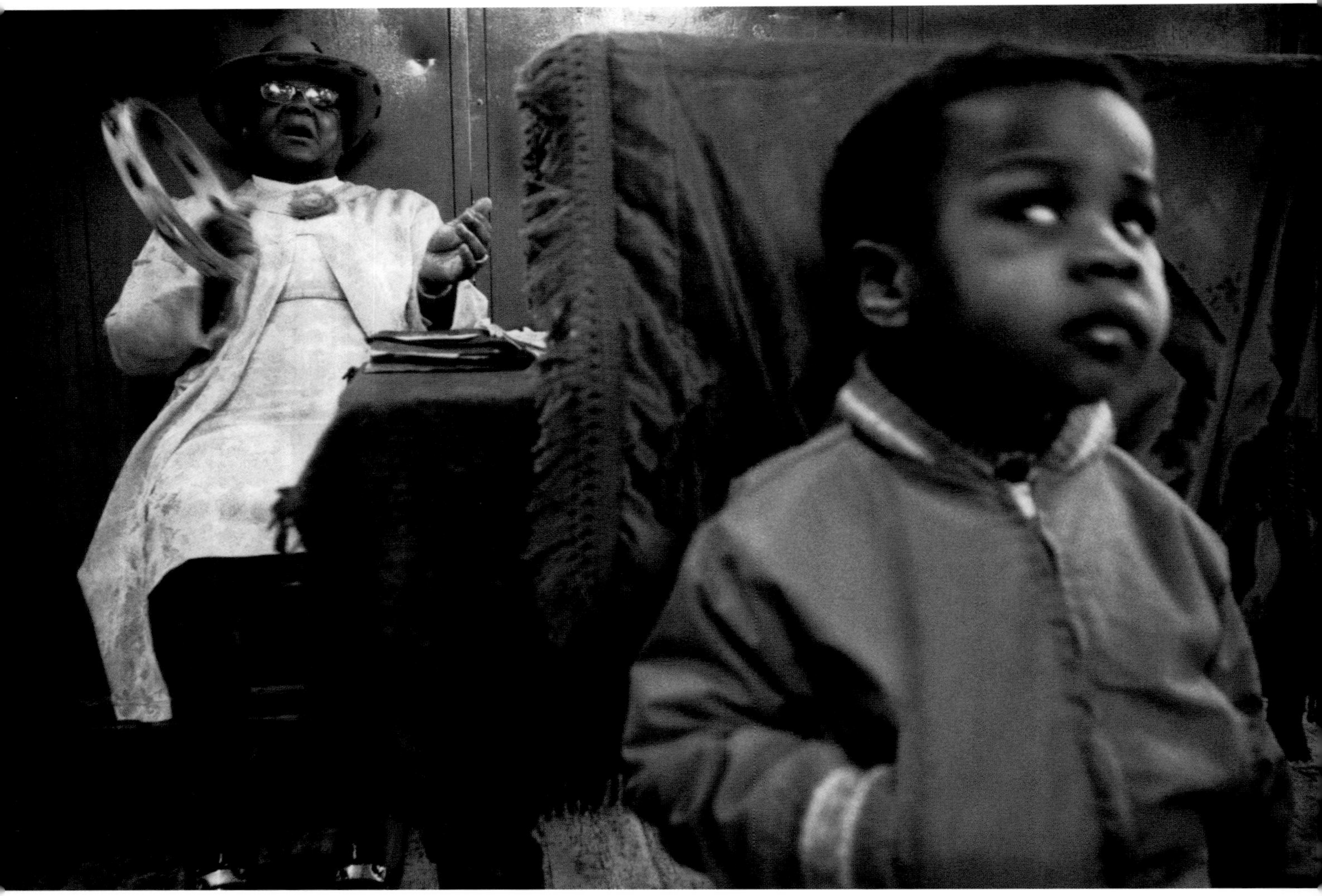

56. Preacher and child, Brixton church, London. 1976

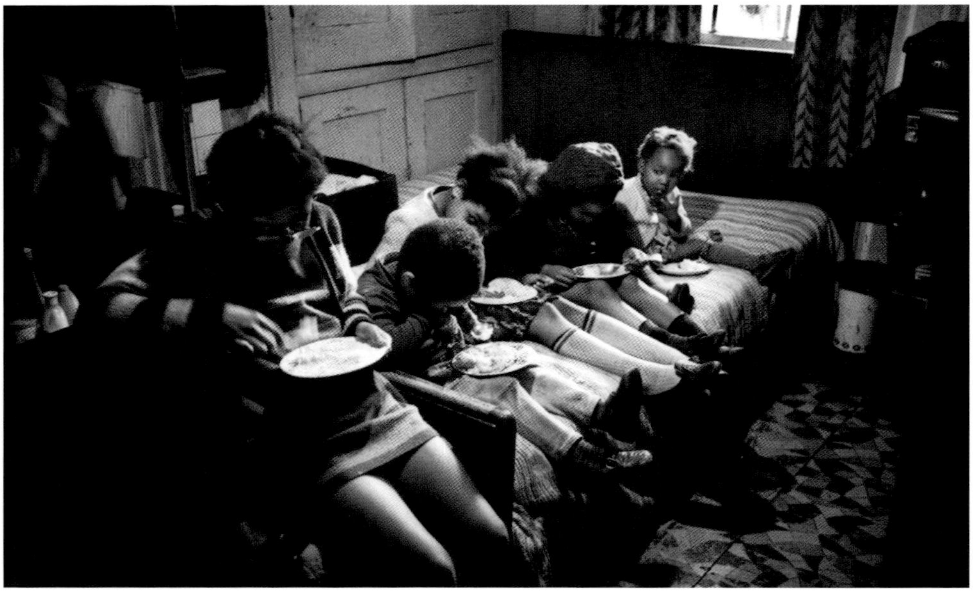

57. Kids eating on bed, immigrant's home, Brixton, London. 1976

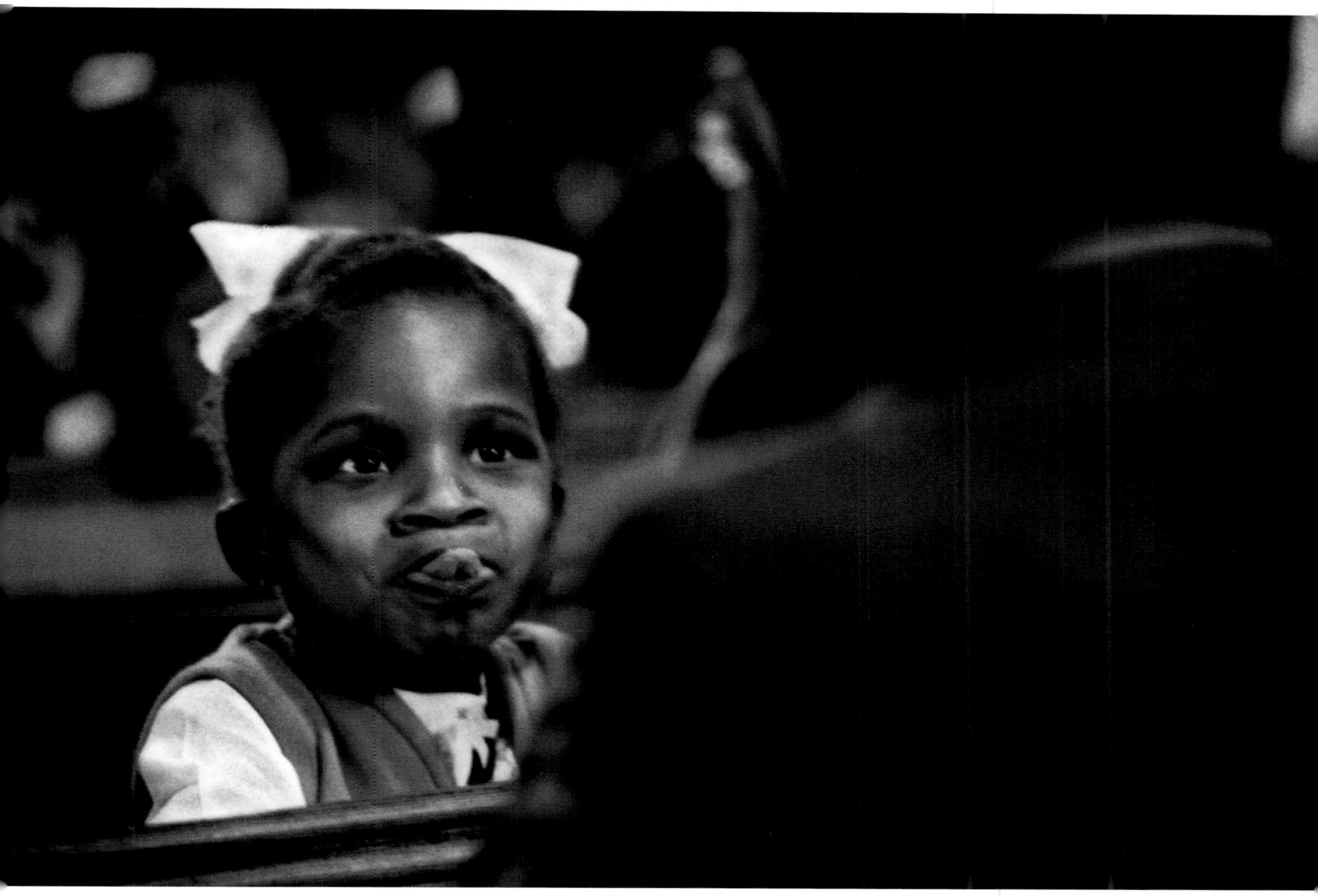

58. Child, tongue and Sunday School teacher, Brixton church, London. 1976

Black, yellow, white or red would eat each other's bread.
Workers would own the product of their hands.
Peasants would possess their land held dear.
Work itself would be shared,
eased by electronics and rationality,
its every action transformed
into a celebration of creativity.

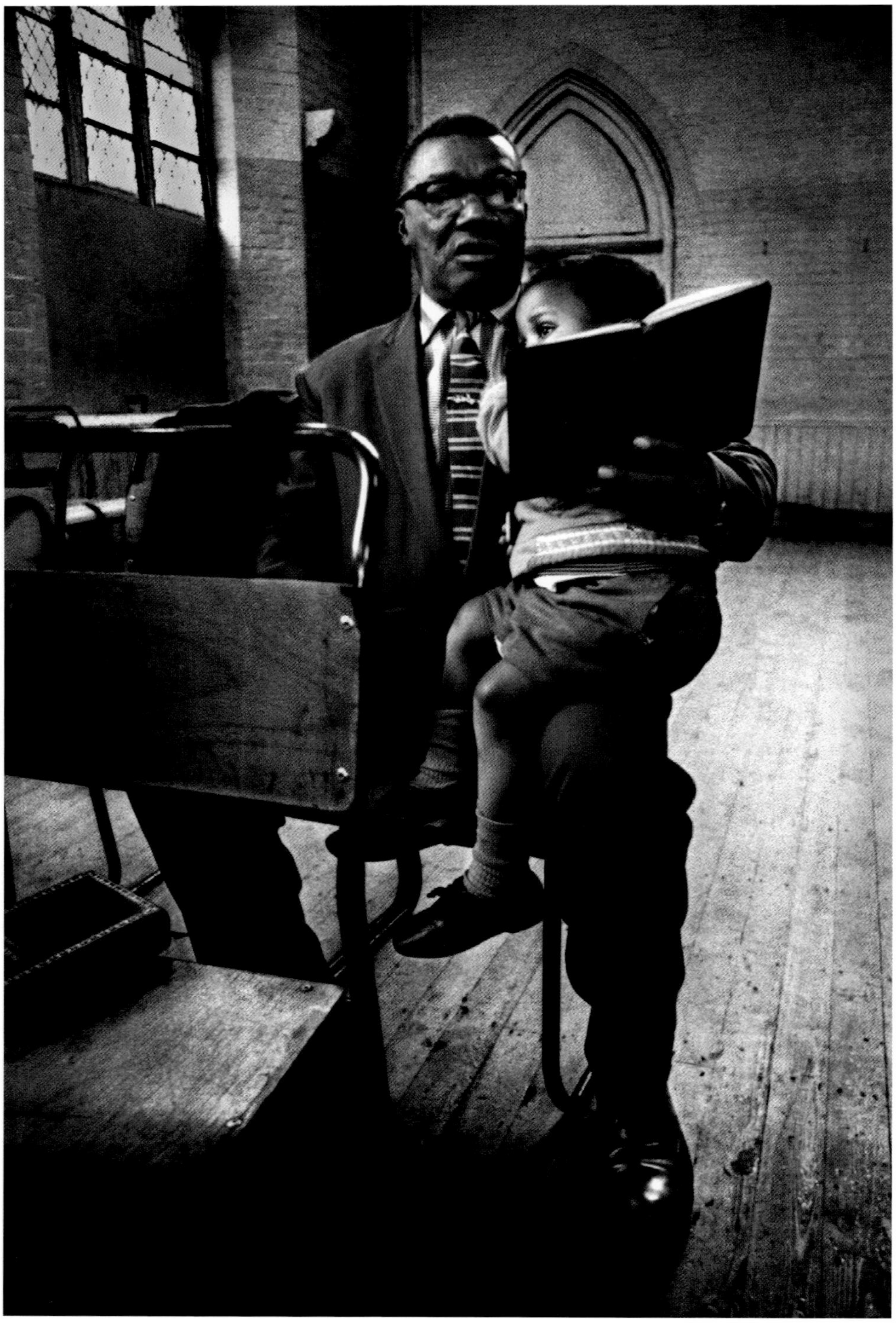

59. Grandfather and child, Brixton Church, London. 1976

60. Man looks into pub, Brixton, London. 1976

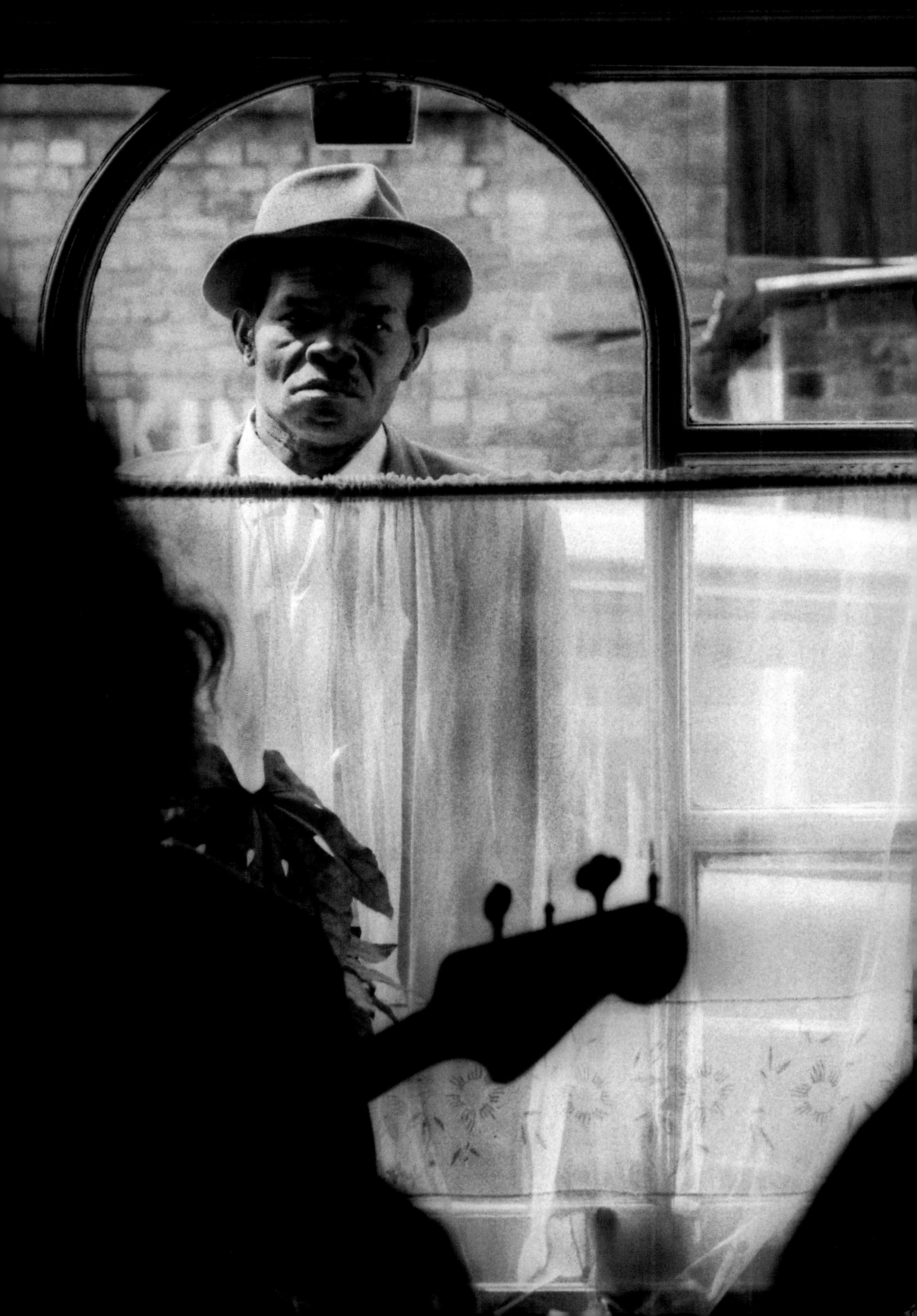

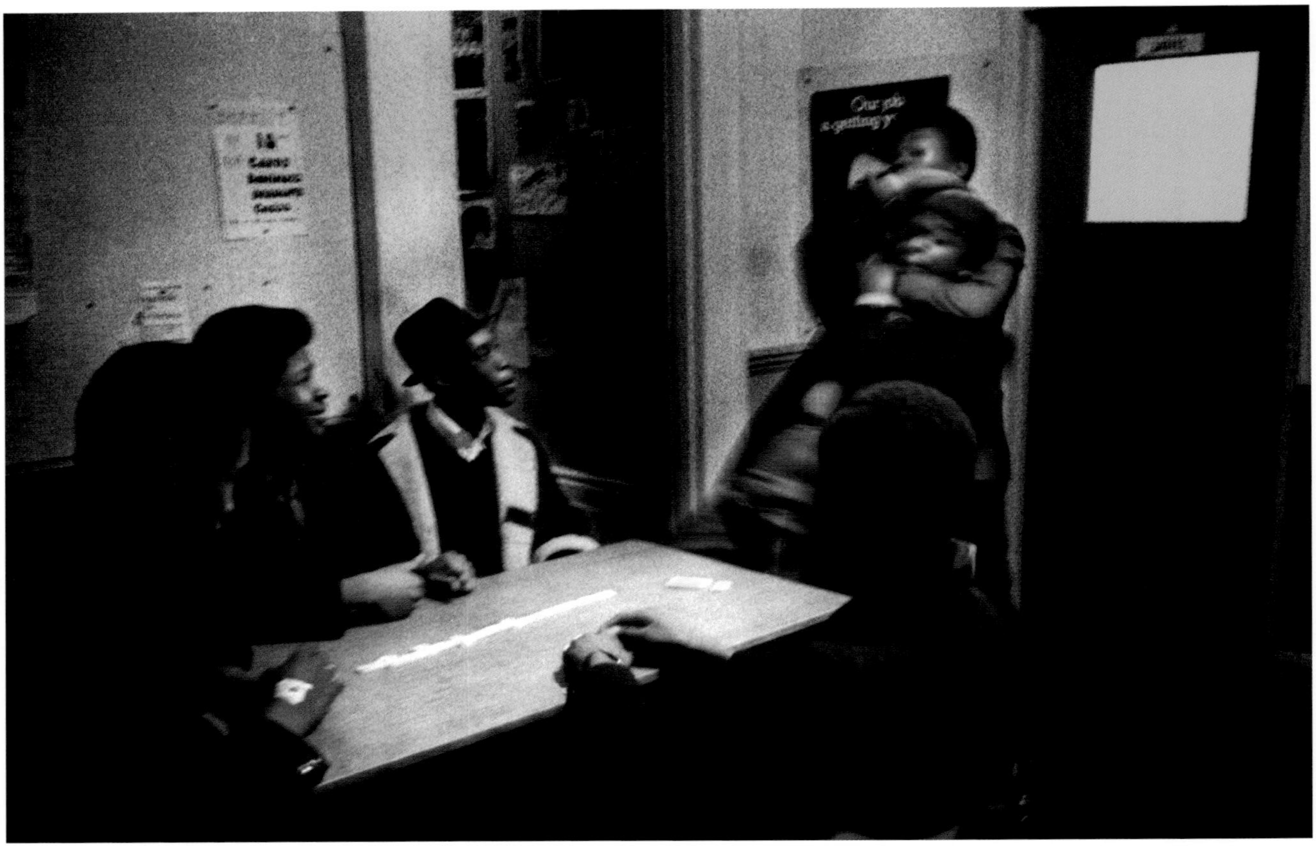

61. Fighting over dominoes, youth club, London. 1971

As a kid I knew only what had been told to me
and what I had seen.
But I sensed deep in the cortex of dreams
a richer distant life.
As most kids, I lived inside a narrow world ...
a world reproduced in these kids lives above ...
we owned similar pain.

62. Woman during service, Brixton church, London. 1976

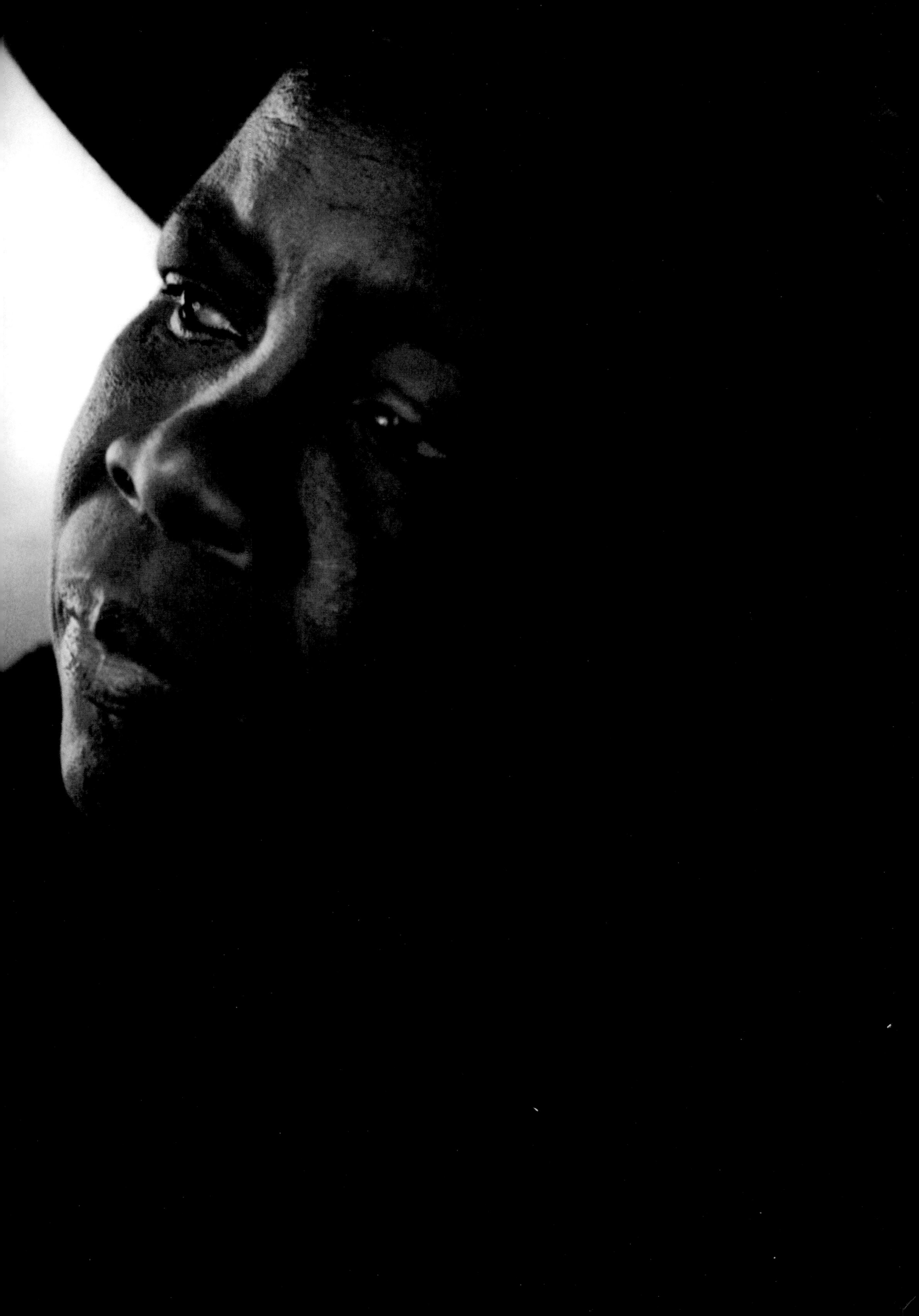

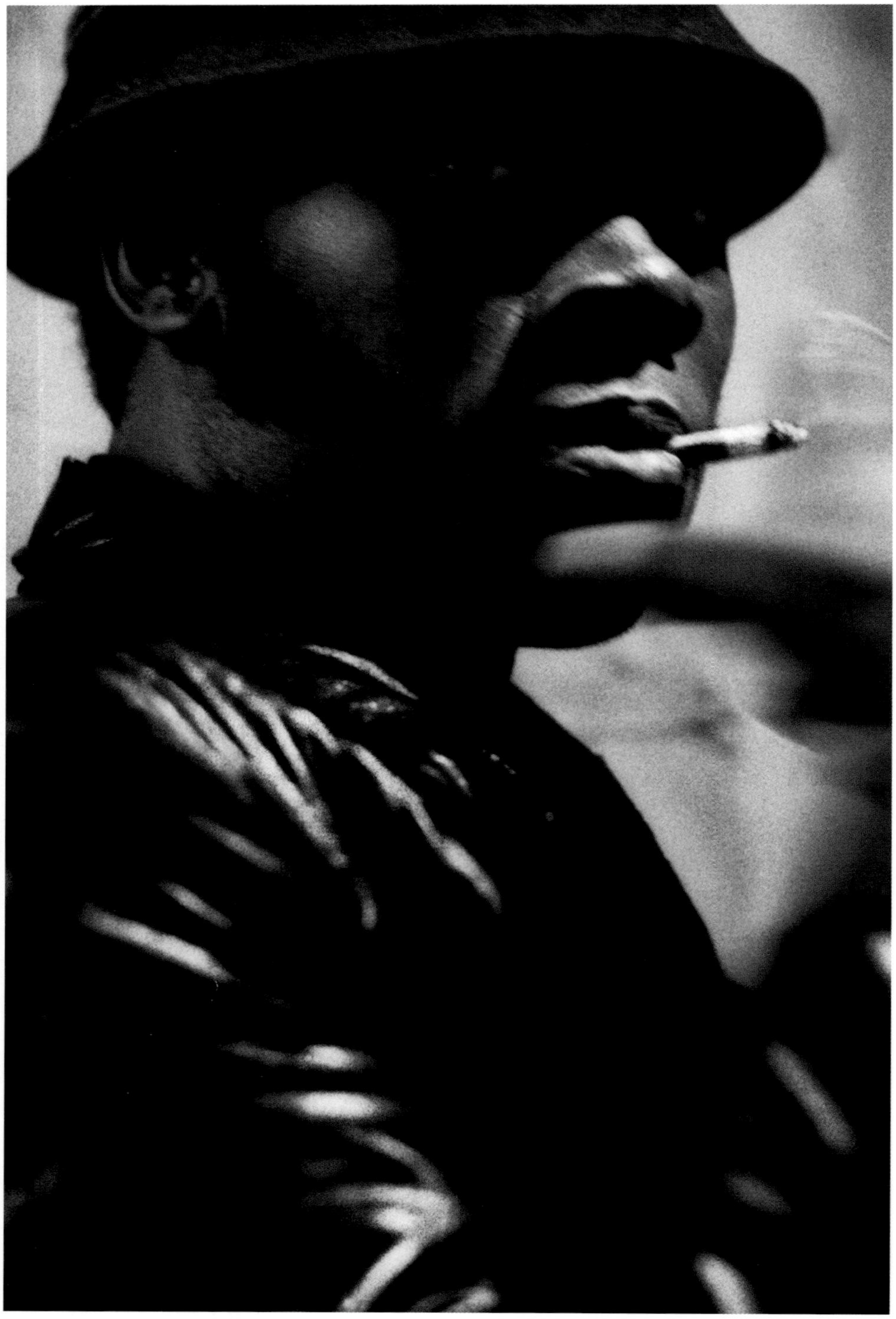

63. Youth jerking his thumb, youth club, Harlesden, London. February 1971

64. Couple in clinch, wedding party, Harlesden, London. August 1977

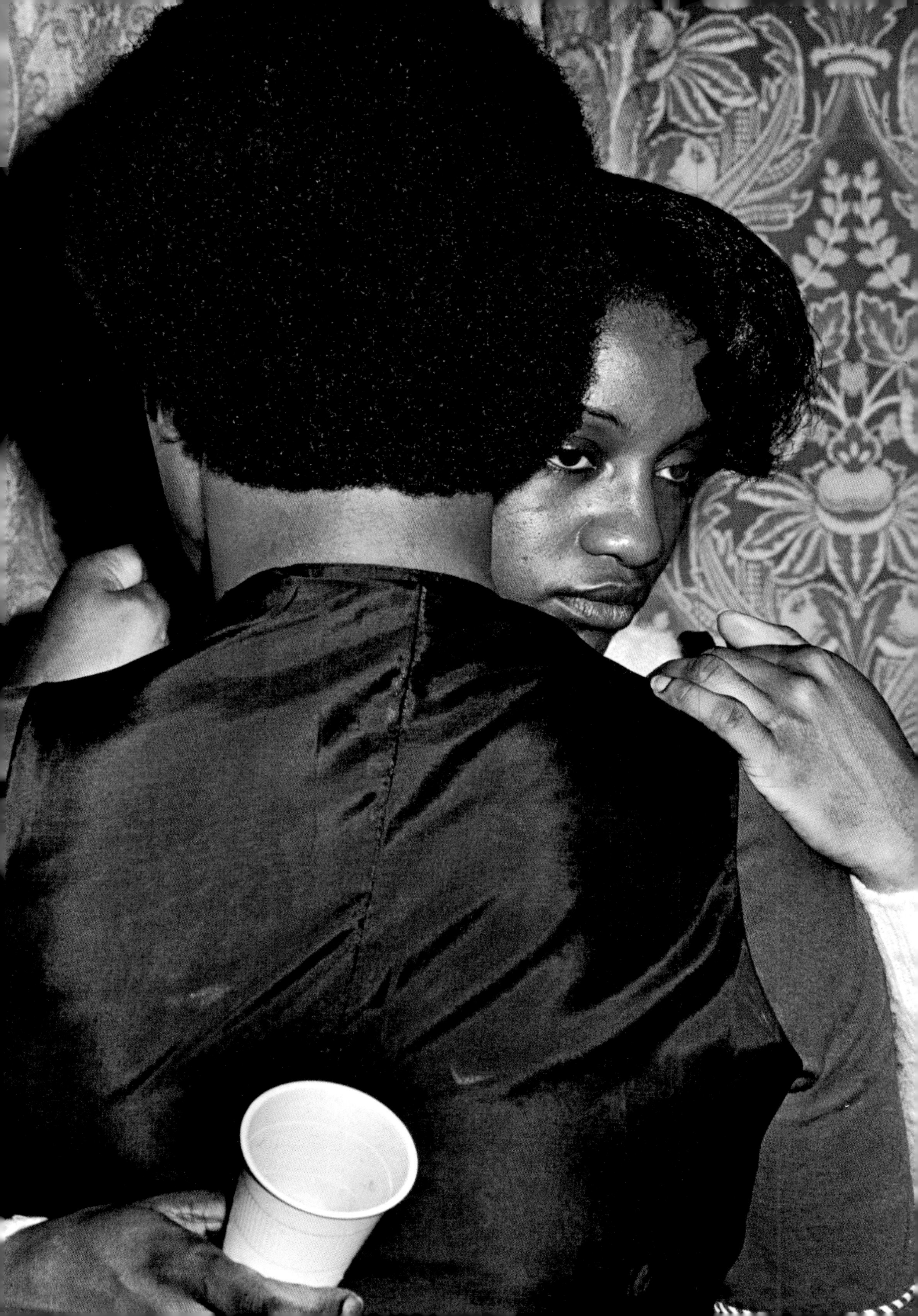

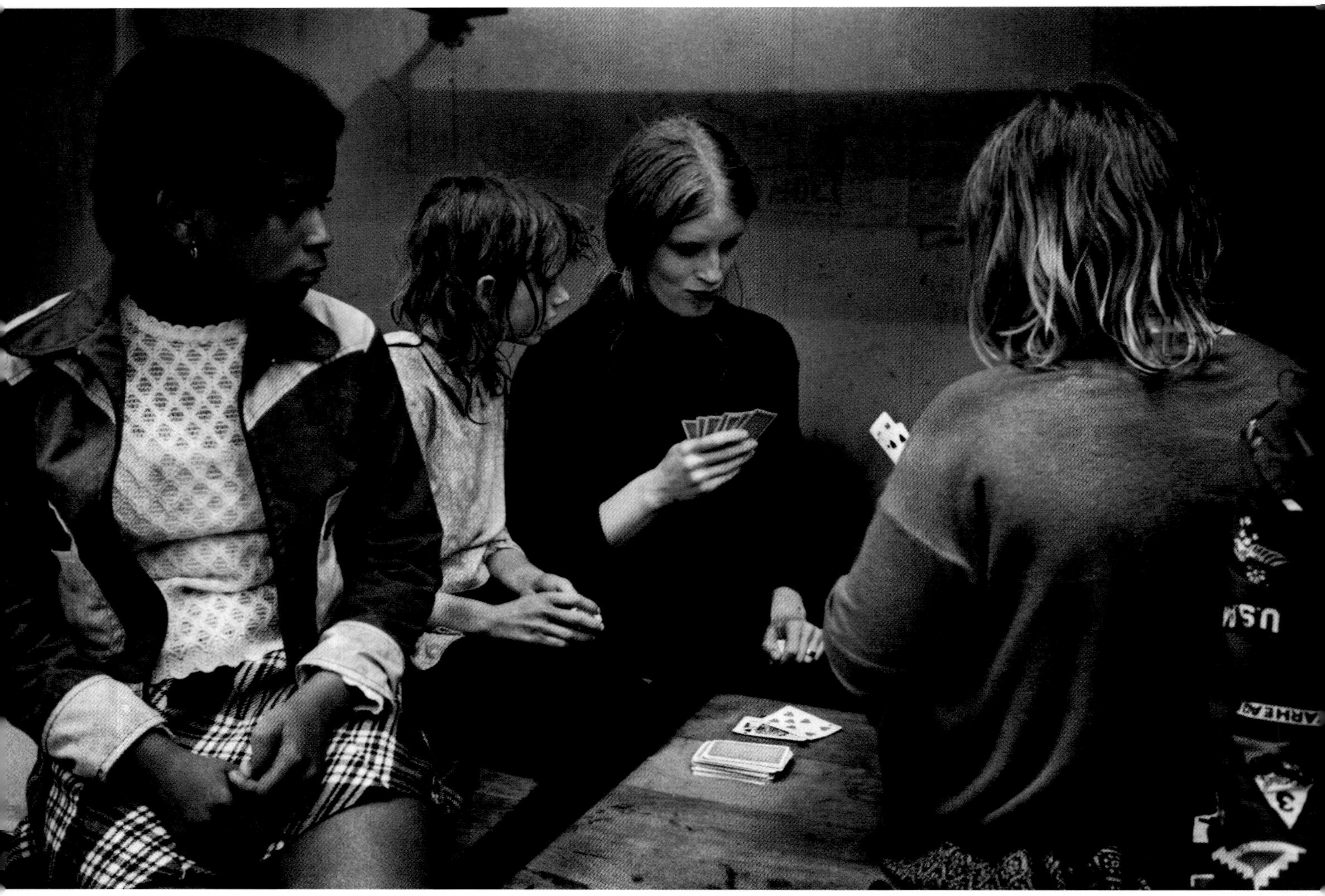

65. Card game, East London youth club. Summer 1972

Without a dream we have no place in history:
yesterday exists to be remembered
today is here, just here
and tomorrow is something to imagine.

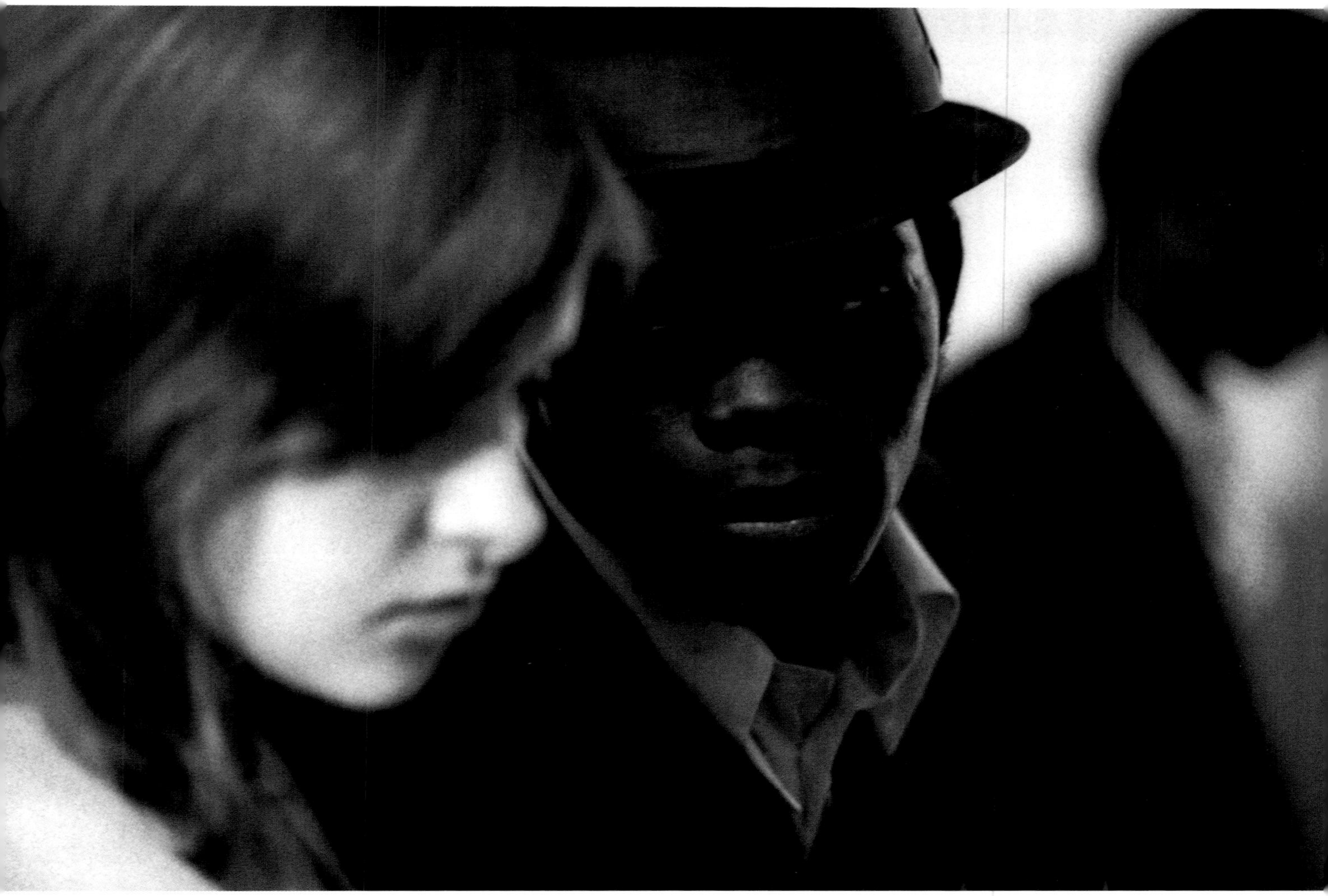

66. Black youth, white girl, youth club, Harlesden, London. February 1971

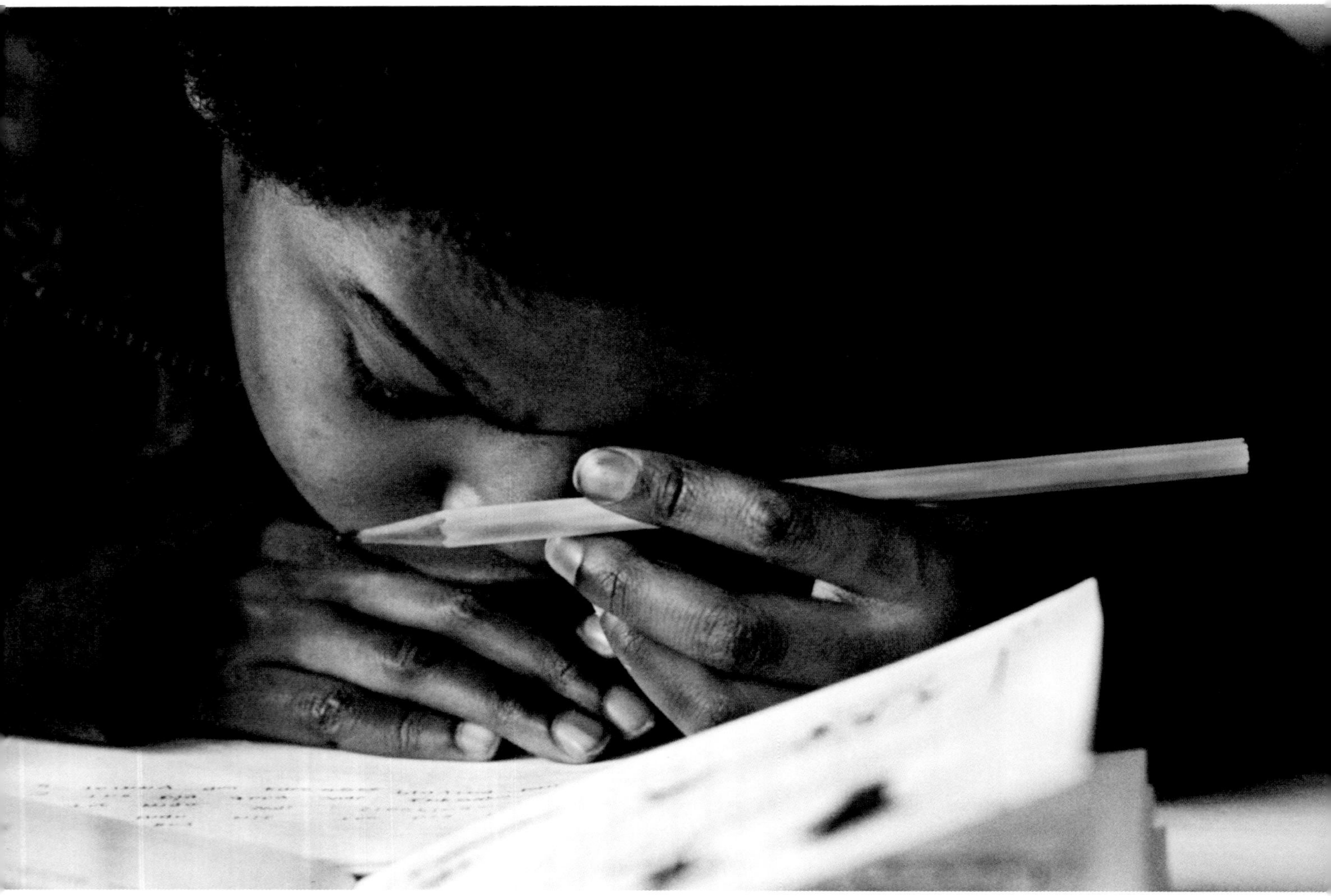

67. Boy struggling with studies, special Saturday School for West Indian children, Harlesden, London. January 1979

Bruce Davidson showed me how the photo-essay as a presentation of others' lives and of one's own concerns and obsessions was socially valuable. But he also made me question the photojournalist as a visitor to others' lives. Are we emotional, aesthetic tourists?

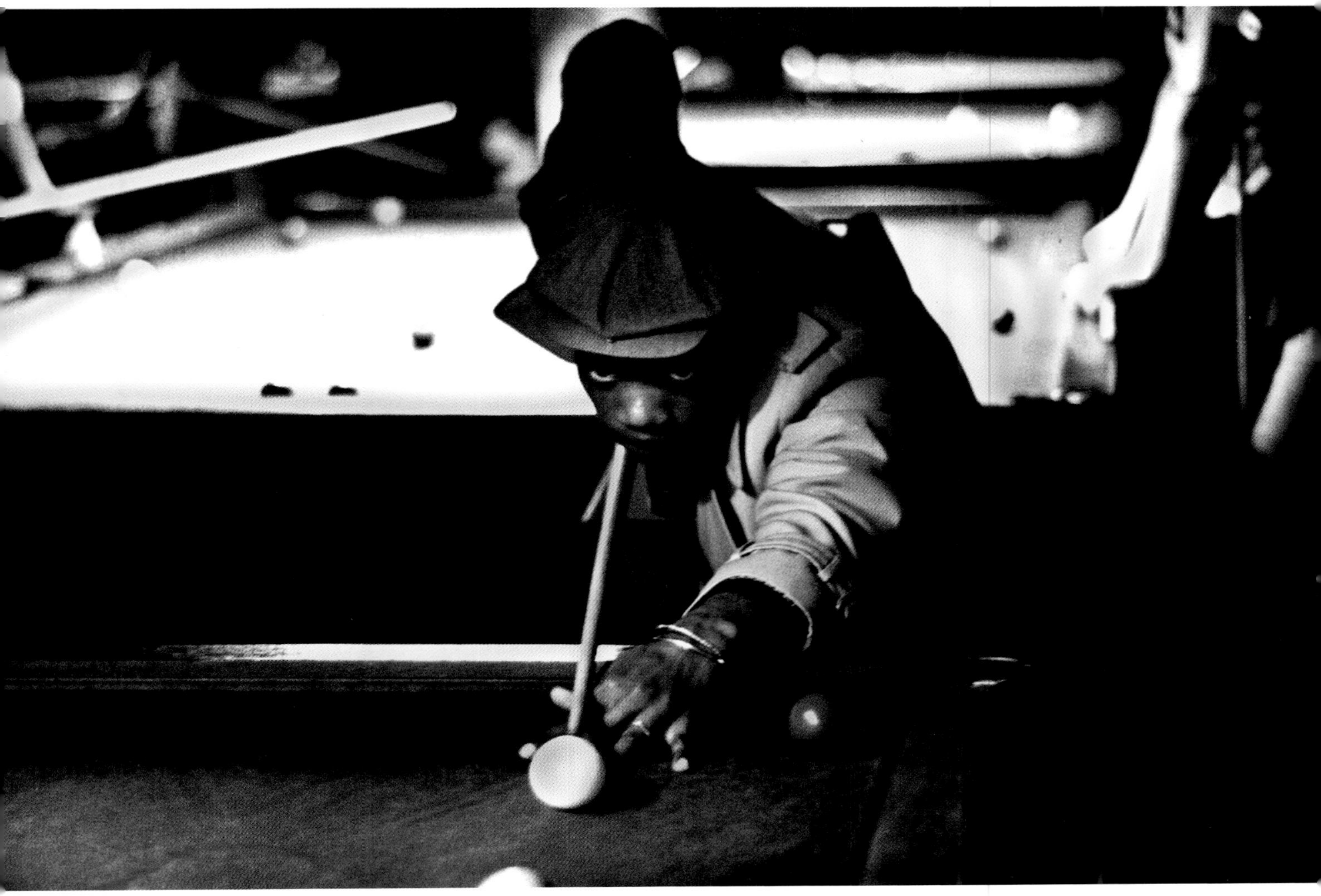

68. Youth playing pool, Harlesden, London. February 1971

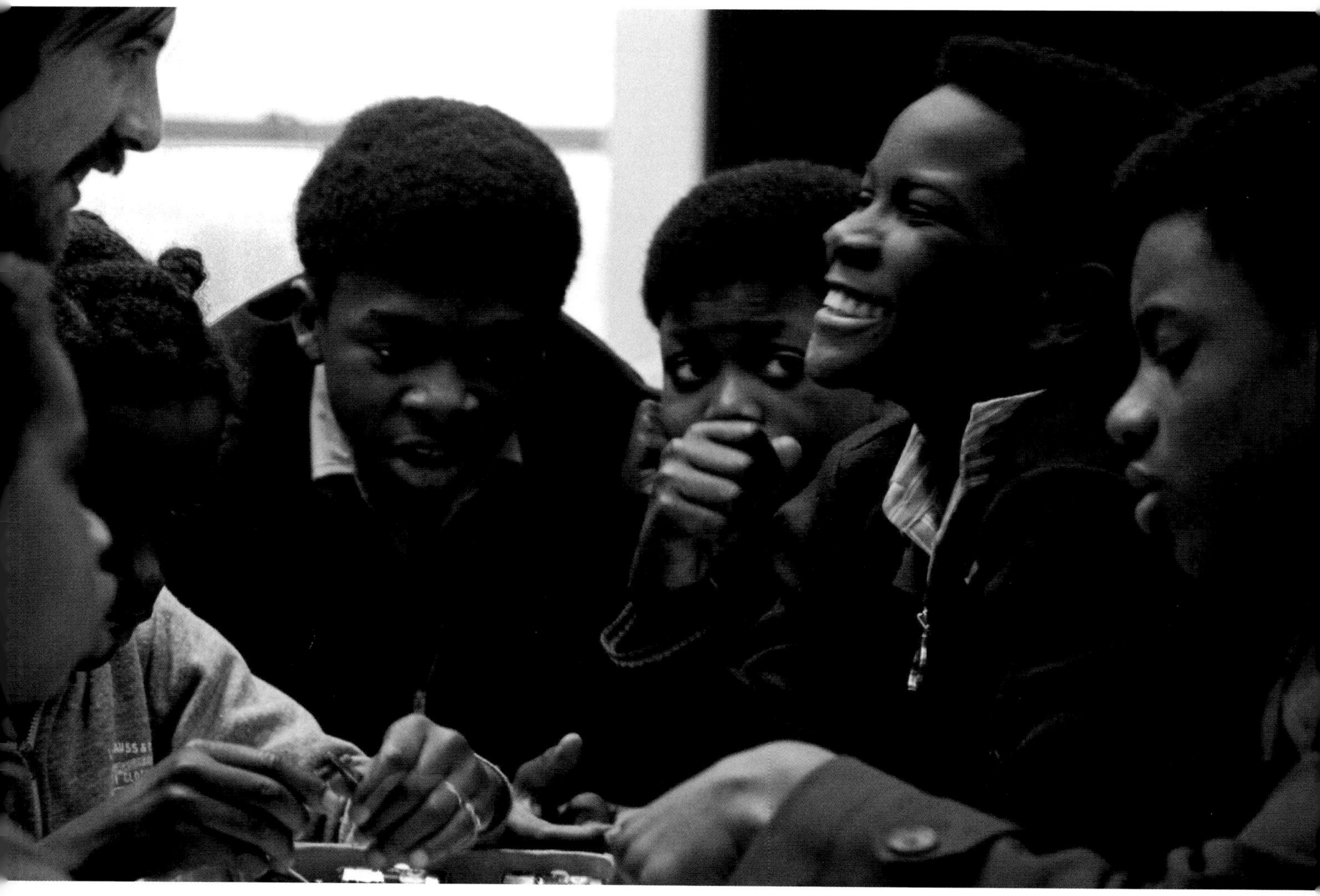

69. Pupil makes a discovery, North London. February 1979

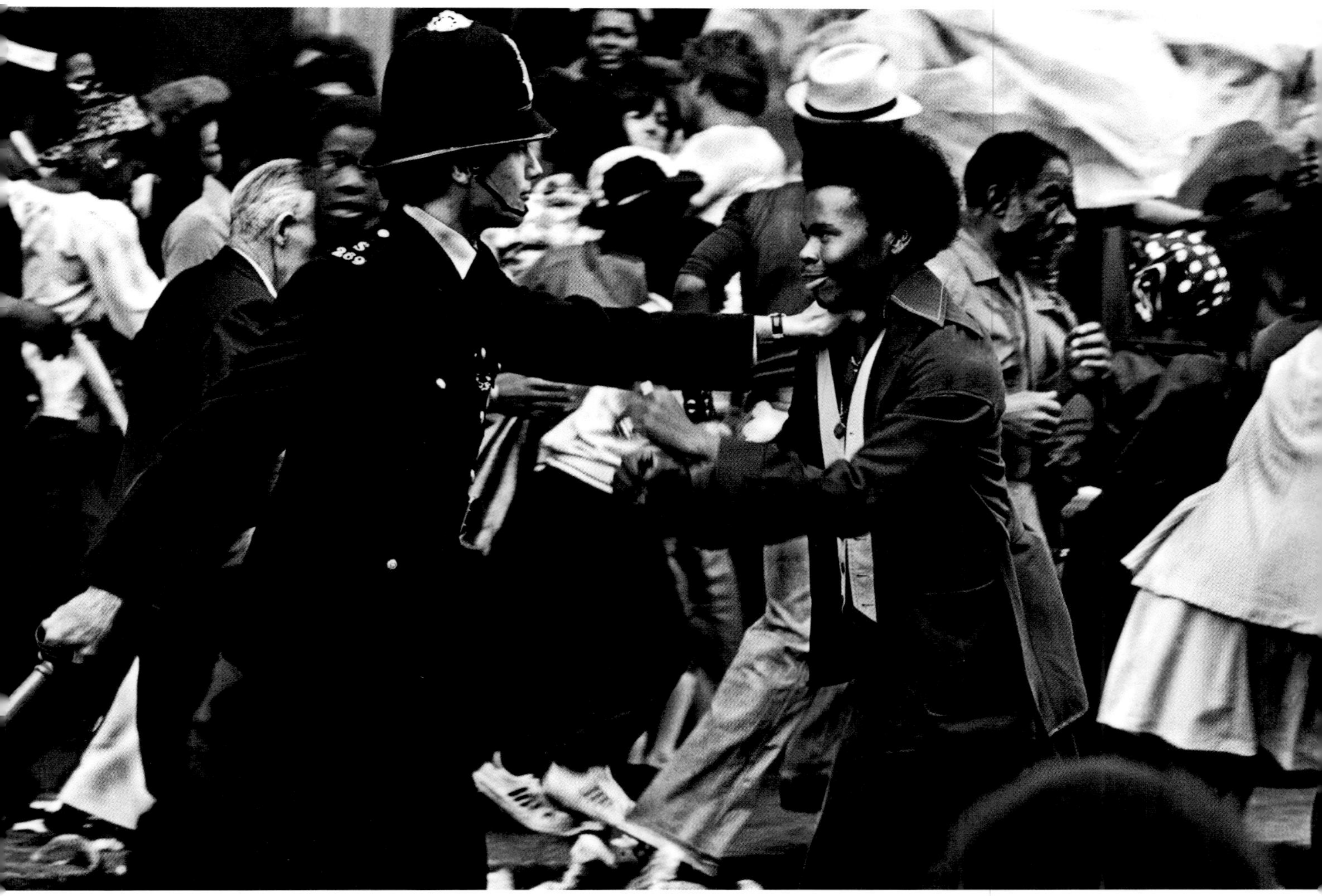

70. Police riot, Notting Hill Festival, London. August 1977

Robert Capa was an inspiration for bravery
and for serving progressive social needs with the camera.
He taught me about the need to be in there,
a tendency later revealed by David Douglas Duncan and Don McCullin,
and his images showed me not to flinch at key emotional moments.

RESISTANCE

OBJECTIVE:

Throughout the 1970s factory after factory was closed down. Wanting a scapegoat, the press accused the unions of destroying the economy when they demanded no redundancies and decent wages. Then they accused foreign workers of being responsible. Finally they demonised the unemployed as scroungers living off the state. But resistance arose throughout industry. In the mid 1970s a core of the Socialists Workers Party created the Right To Work Campaign. After many demonstrations they formed a march of the unemployed from Manchester to London. Under rain and constant police harassment they arrived at the outskirts of London. Police busses blocked side roads, motorcycle police cruised alongside the marchers and when they found themselves in front of a police station, three policemen tried to snatch the leader. This led to many marchers, including young women, being beaten to the ground, dragged off and arrested. But the next day a huge rally at the Royal Albert Hall went ahead. Eventually many marchers were jailed. Unemployment peaked at around five million, affecting up to 25 per cent of the population. By 1983 production had fallen to 30 per cent of its post-war high. The nation was bruised and divided and Britain was seen as "the poor old man of Europe". This tragedy was an early foretaste of globalization, when First World industry would be destroyed along with jobs, skills and people's homes ... in order to create a "free" market.

SUBJECTIVE

In and around the Left of that period I met many high-principled people – but I also encountered didactic, paranoid self-seeking narrow-minded bigots and especially philistines who sneered at anything they did not understand, including and especially beauty. It was disheartening to witness this and made me question how such good ideas and intentions could attract such disingenuous people. Only later have I come to understand what these people were ... fundamentalists suffering from "my view is the only view" and "anything which diverges is unacceptable". There was no grey in their paradigm of life – things had to be either 100 per cent consistent with their beliefs or they were wrong. This led to a condemnation of those who diverged from the "true line" and to the miscreant being seen as "other". And otherness, as we know, leads to dehumanisation and from there, terror and murder are not far away.

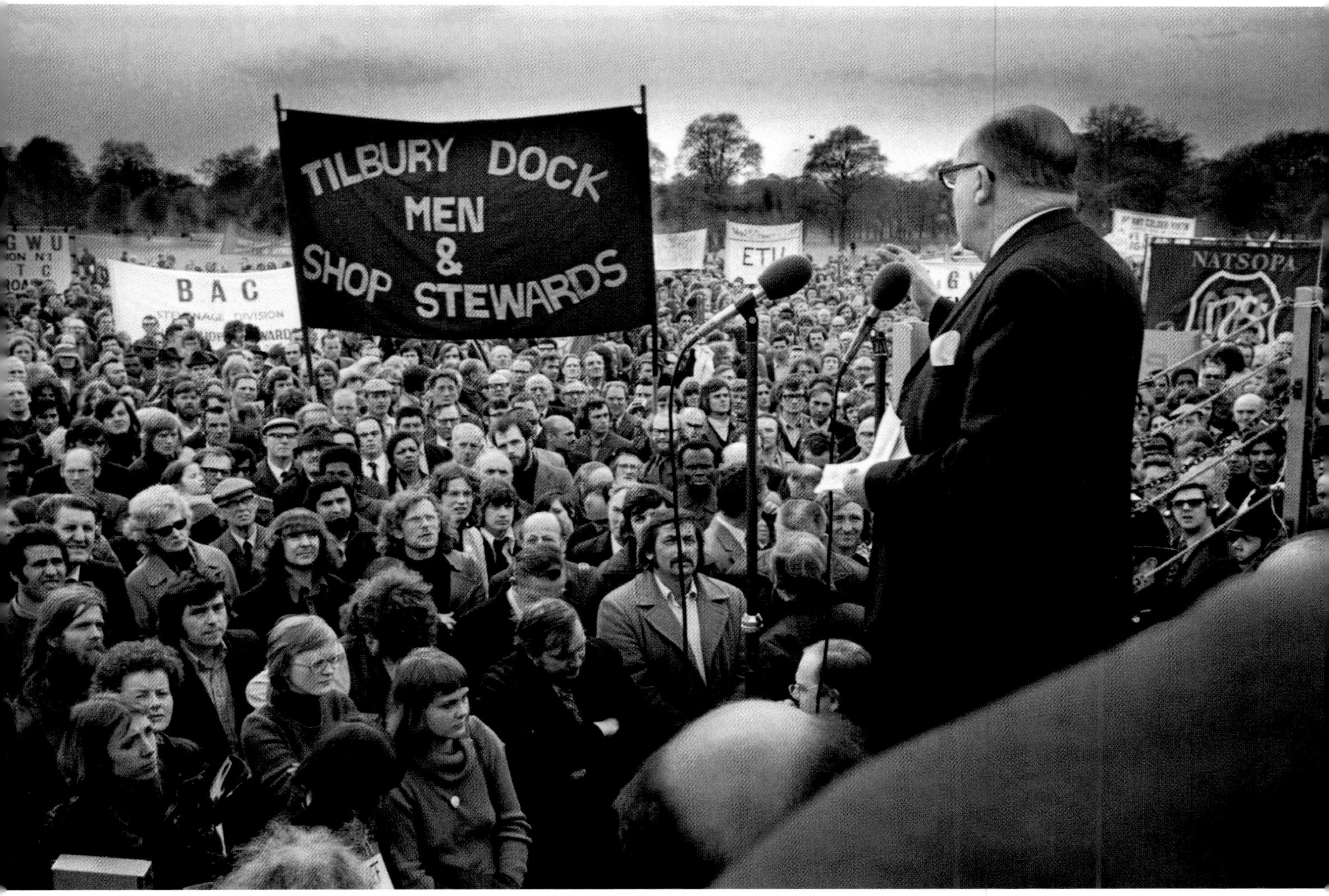

71. Speaker, May Day Trades Union Demonstration, Hyde Park, London. May Day 1973

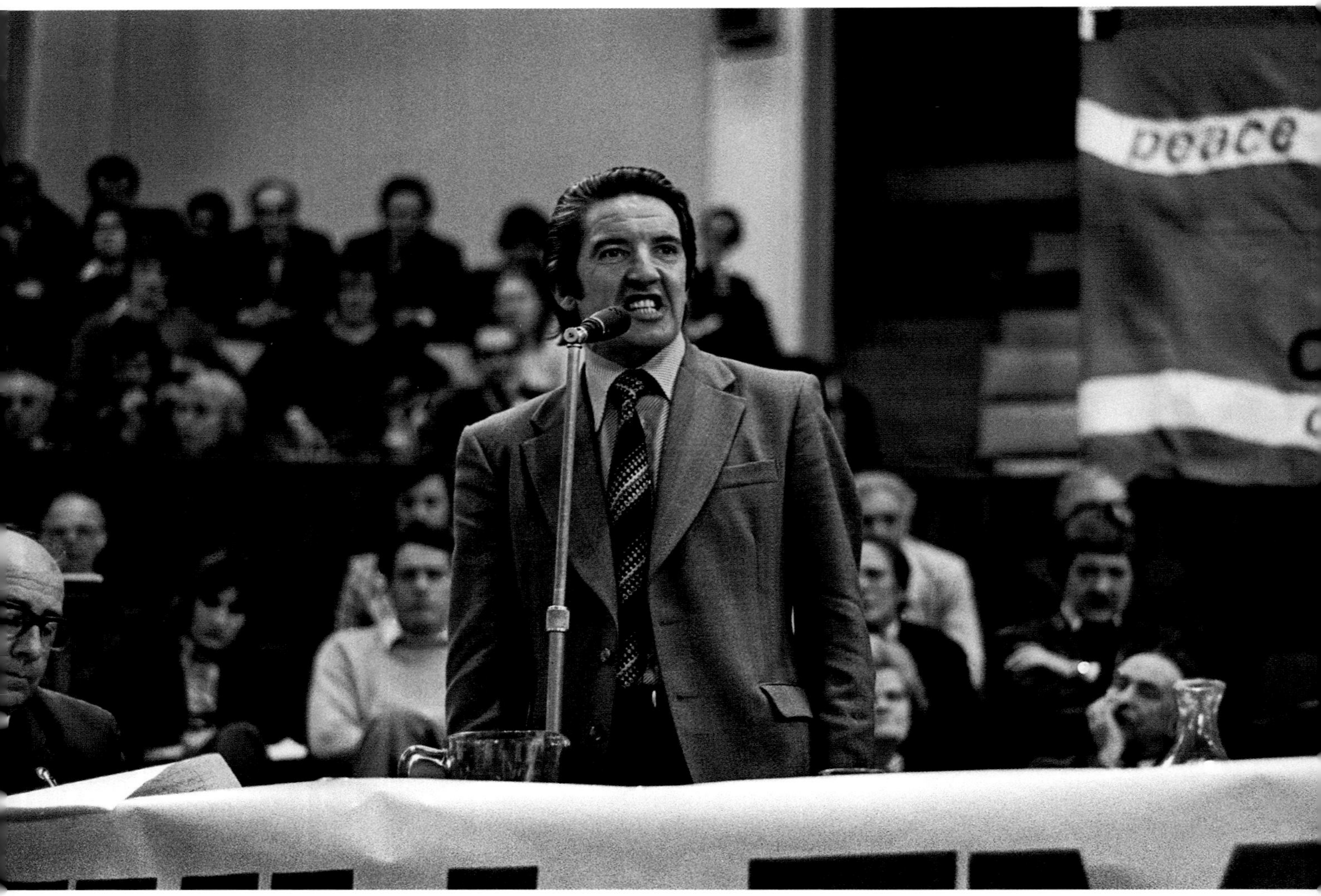

72. Denis McShane, MP, speaking at a Communist Party Unemployment Conference, London. 25 March 1976

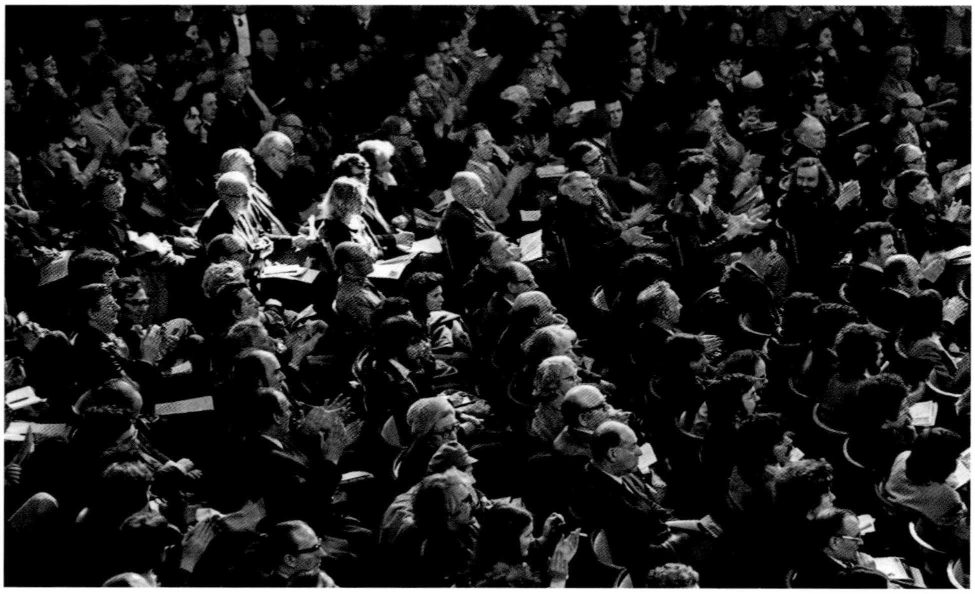

73. Audience, Communist Party Unemployment Conference, London. 25 March 1976

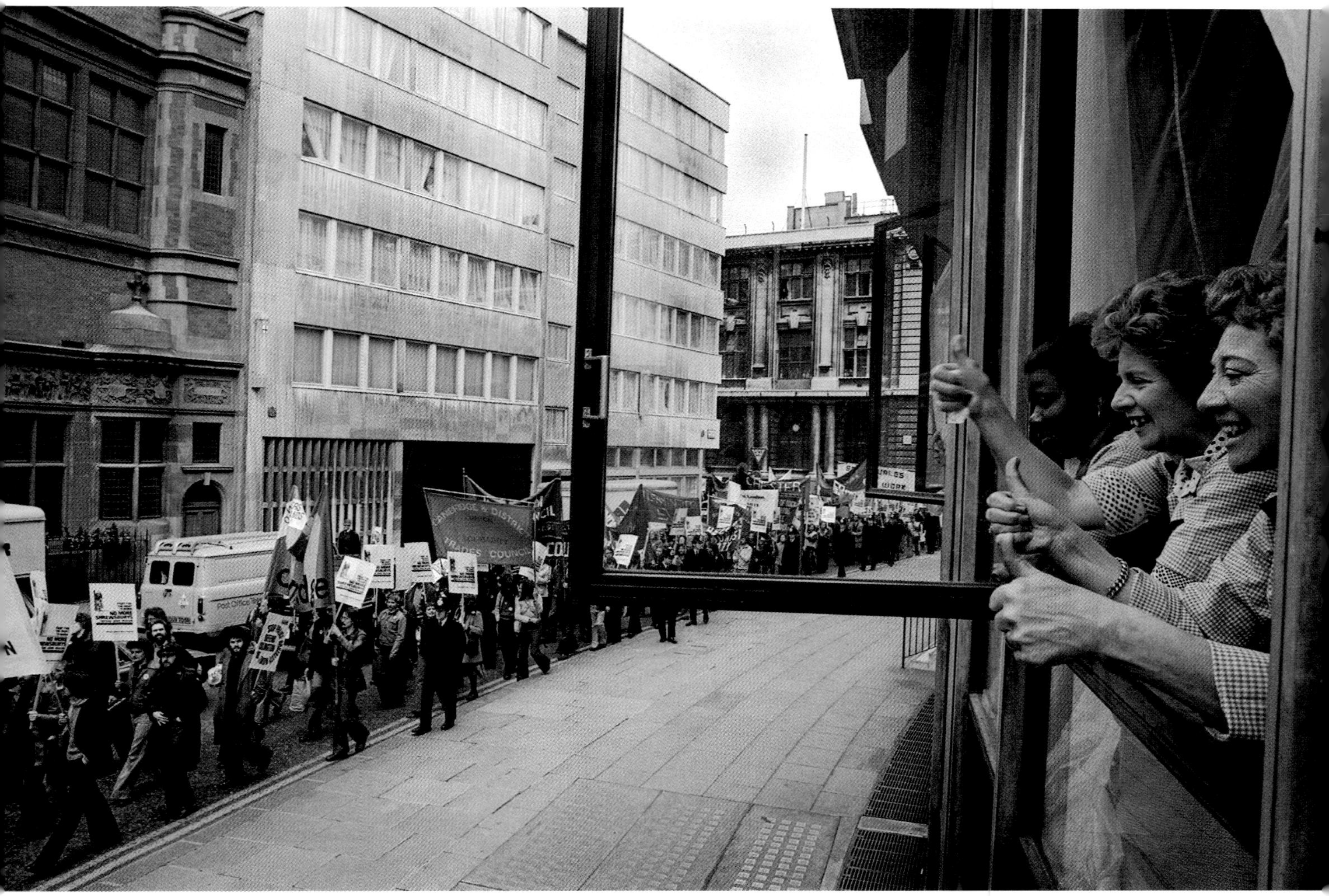

74. Cleaners supporting a trades union demonstration, London. 4 May 1977

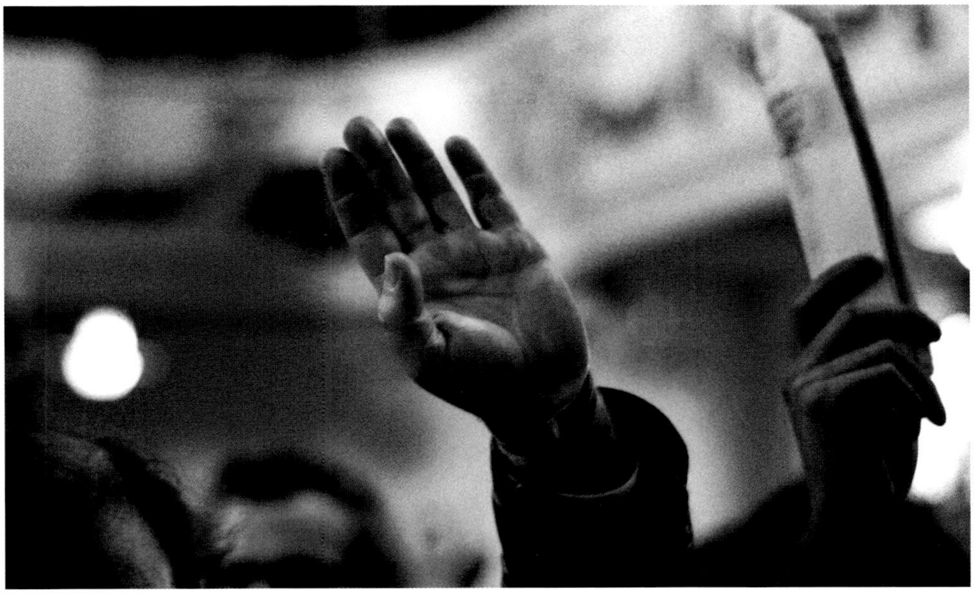

75. Voting, Communist Party Unemployment Conference. 25 March 1976

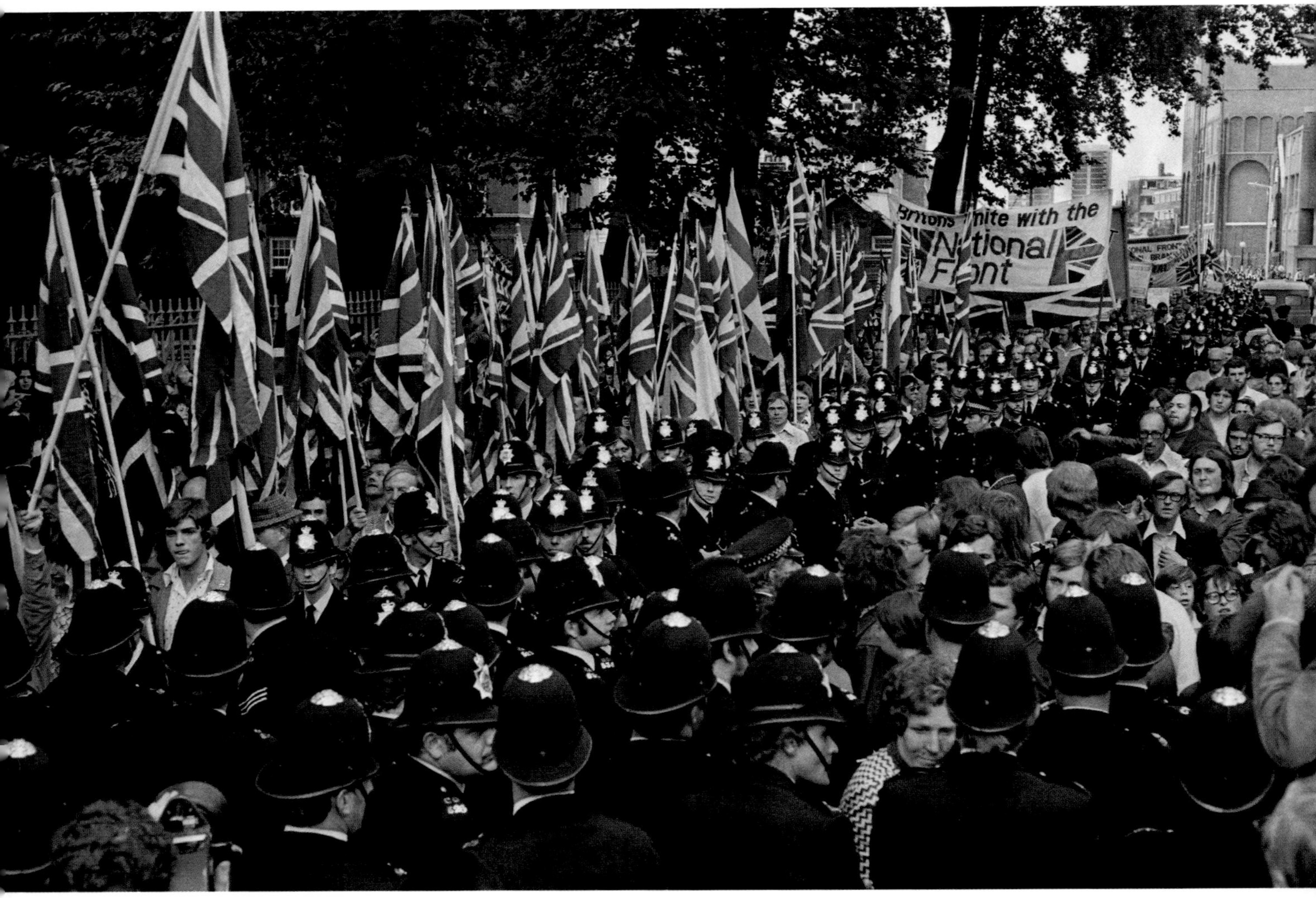

76. National Front racist demonstration, London. September 1975

The Cold War ended, the Berlin wall fell,
the world became post-industrial and post-modern.
Hierarchies were questioned in all areas of life including image making.
I saw the new images on MTV
and began to question the canons of my own work.

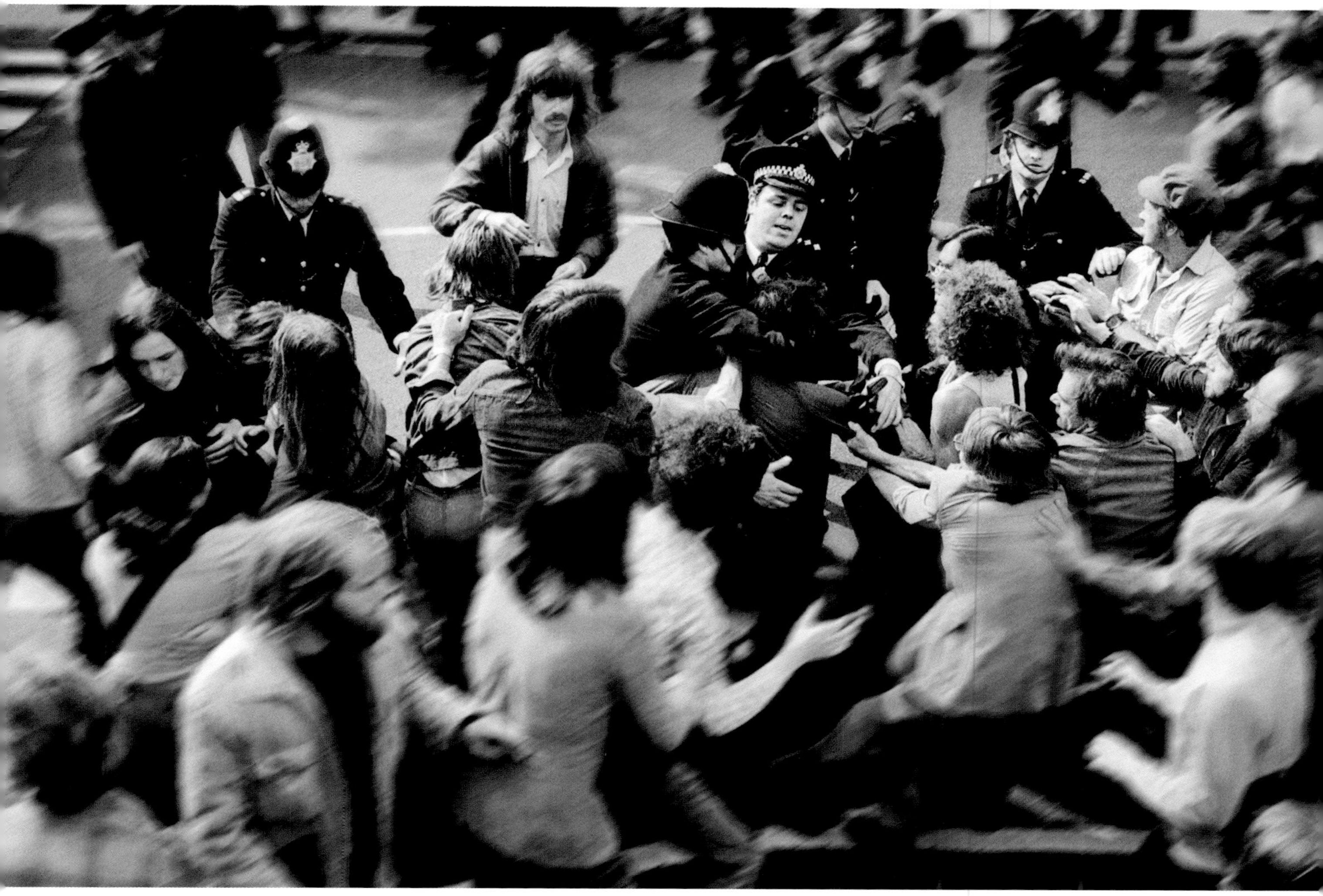

77. Anti National Front demonstration, London. September 1973

My youthful concerns returned: questions of human freedom, repression, the need for love, faith, identity and belief.
I began producing images in motion that once I had created in stills.
After 600 commercials I made a feature film.
People asked: "What is the fascination with framing faces so close?"

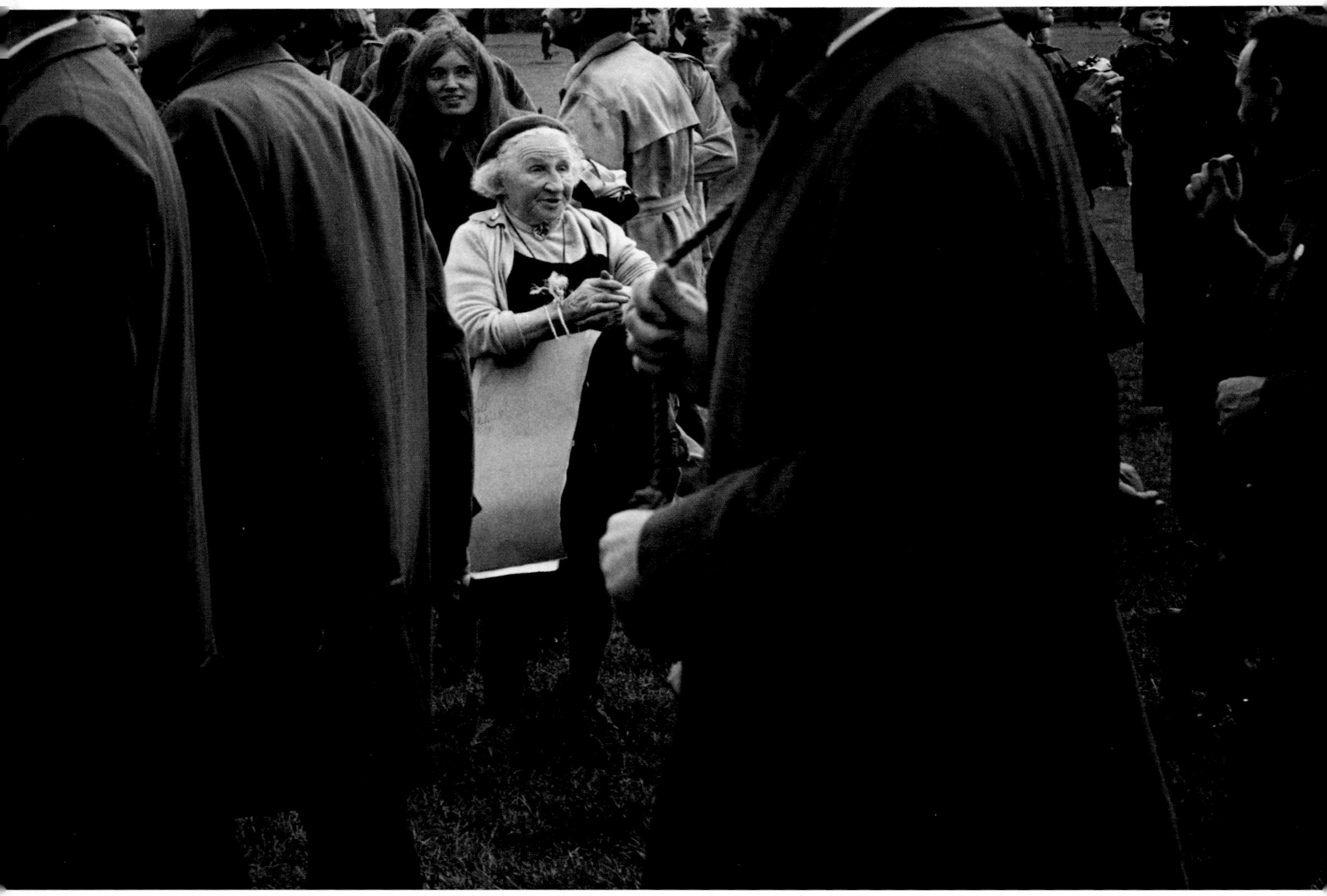

78. Women applauding the march, Trades Union May Day Demonstration, London. 1 May 1973

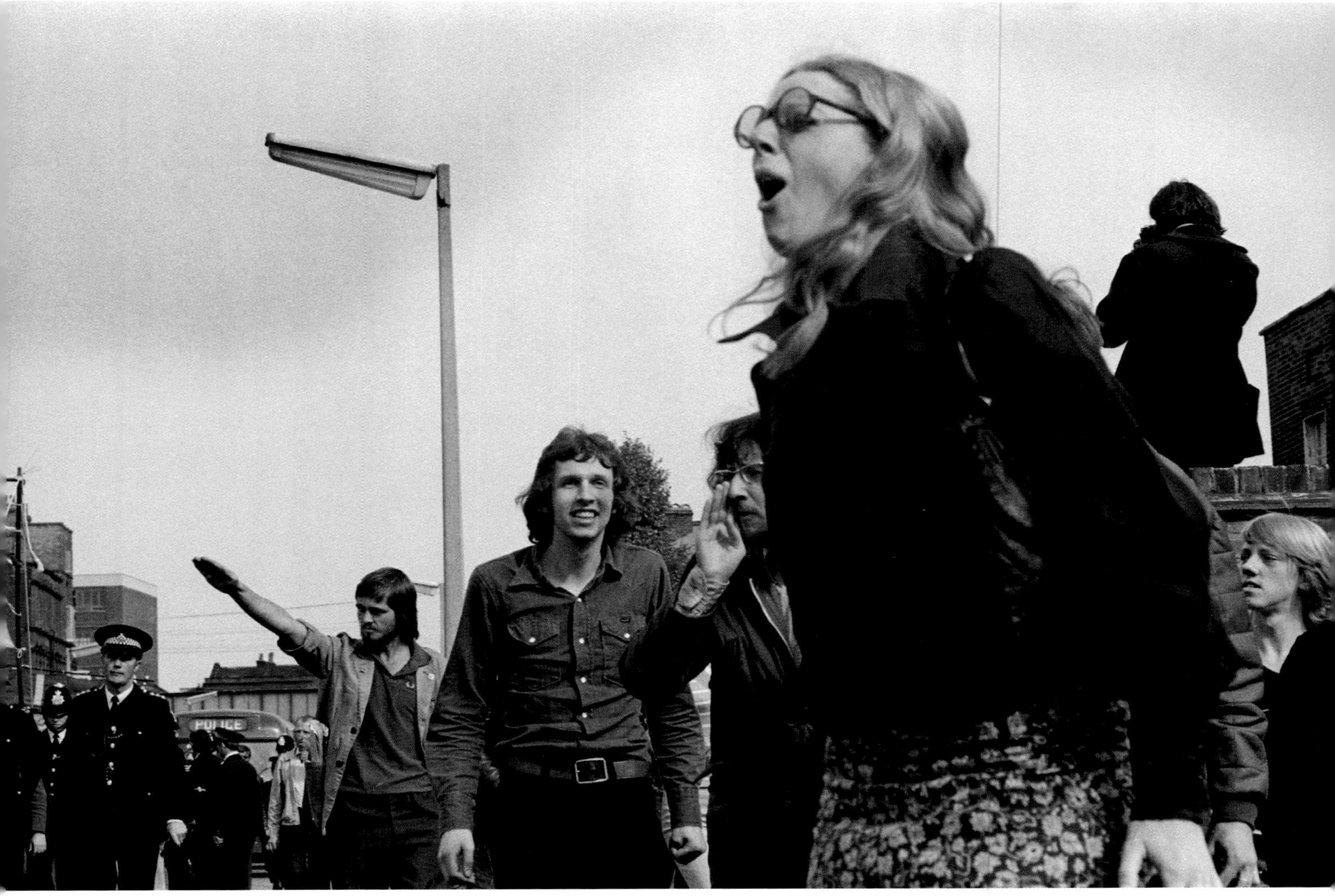

79. A woman taunts Nazi marchers, London. September 1975

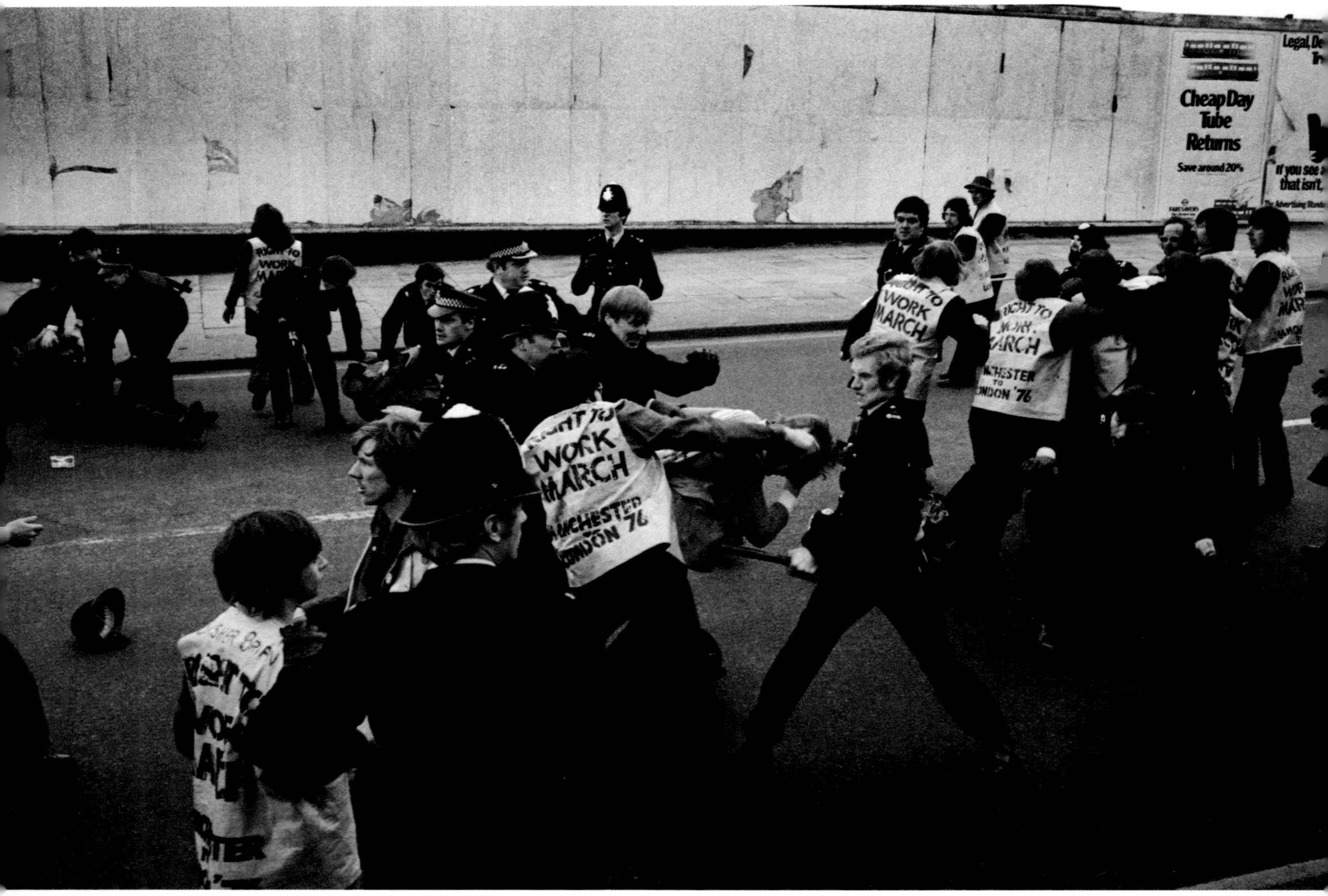

80. Police attempt to stop Right to Work Campaign marchers, Staples Corner, London. Spring 1976

One day I saw a photograph
by a well know photojournalist.
A table with a chair pressed for the thousandth time
against the wall behind leaving its mark indelibly in the plaster,
a partly eaten plate of food left in disarray, crumbs –
a portrait of someone outside the frame.

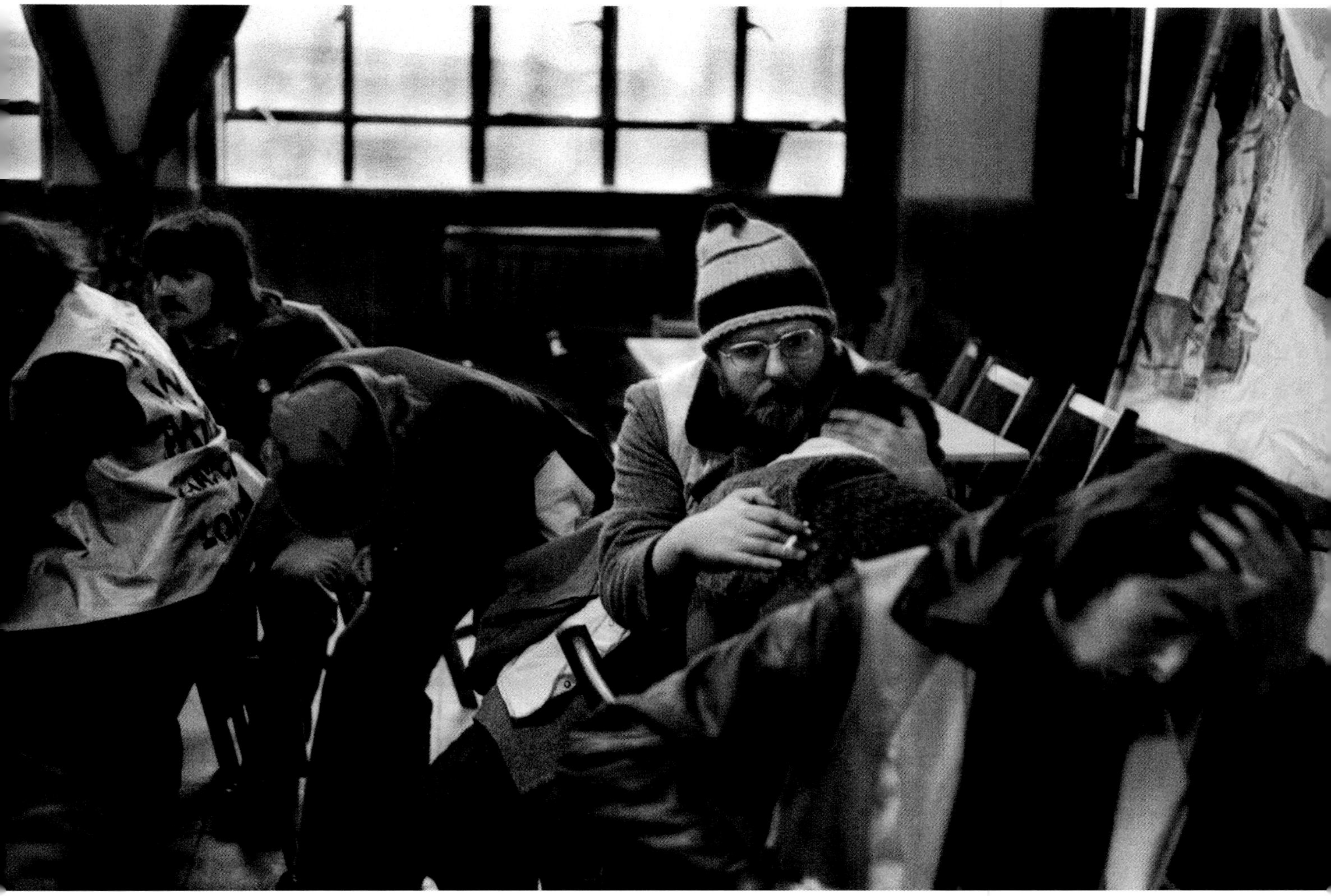

81. Distressed marchers after police attack on the Right To Work Campaign, London. Spring 1976

All those days of cloudy skies,
all those nights of weak tungsten lighting,
all those empty black voids,
all those missed expressions,
missed moments, missed shapes.
It was time for beauty
in a century where so much ugliness had been born.

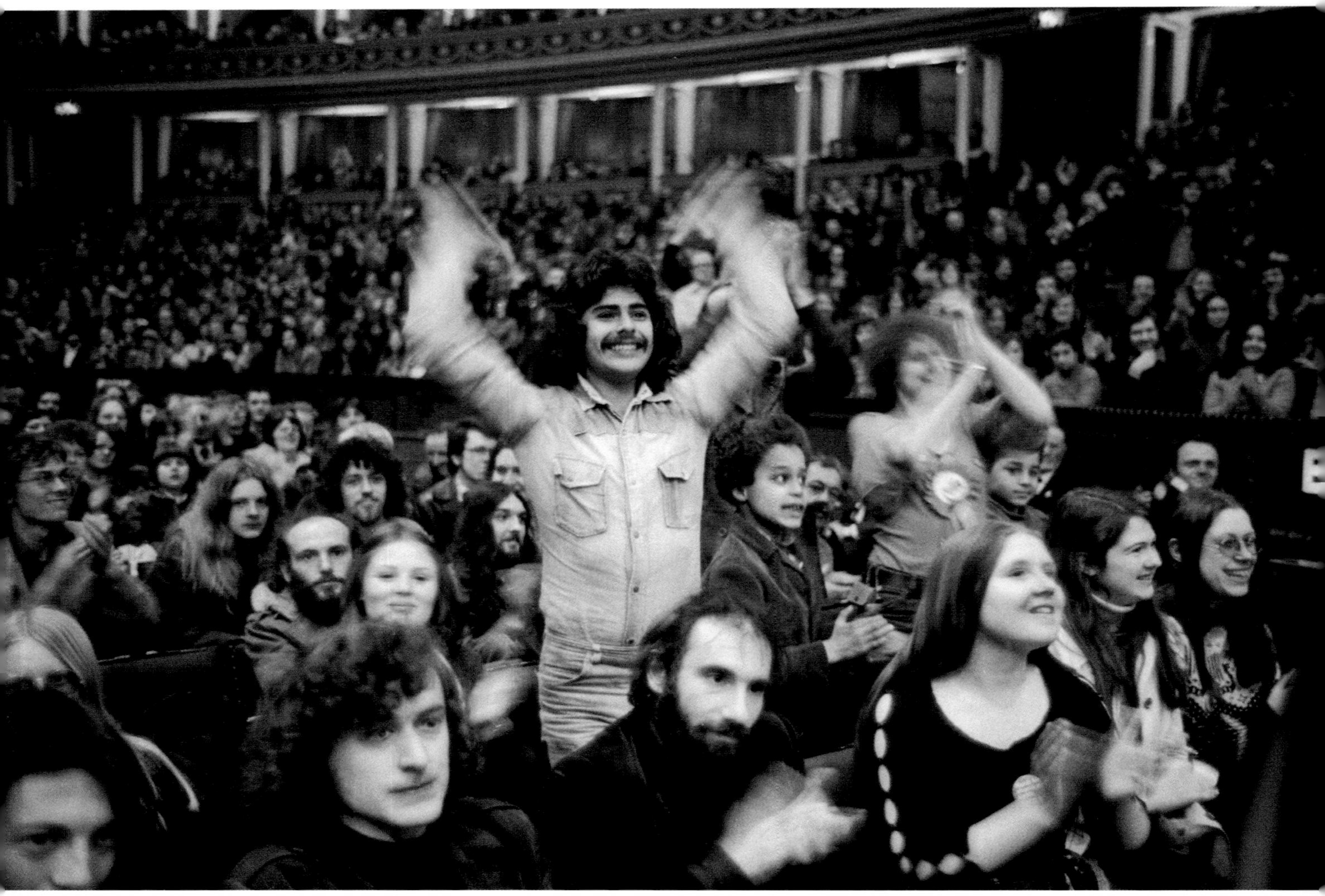

82. The Right To Work marchers greeted in the Albert Hall. March 1976

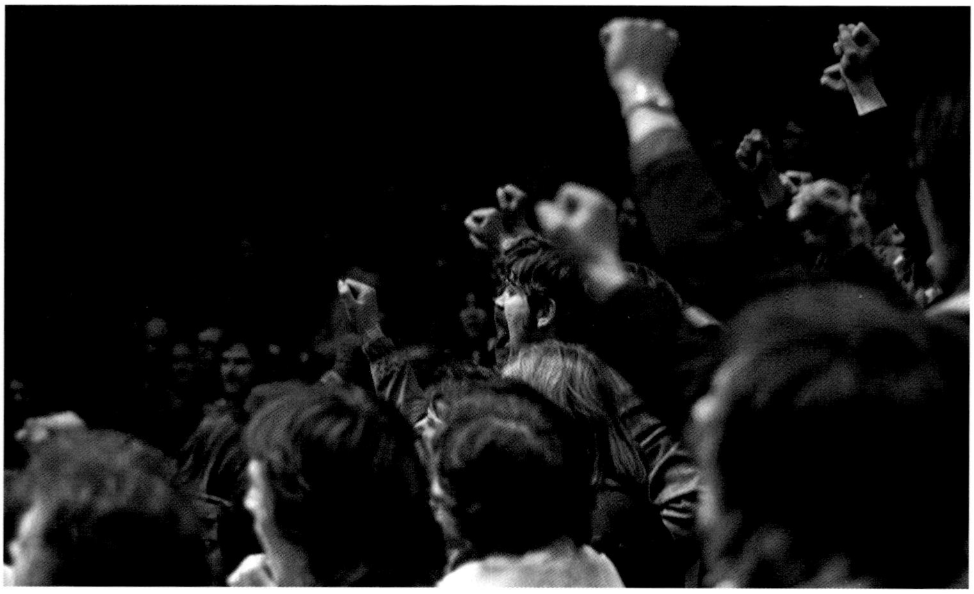

83. The audience raise their fists in solidarity for the Right To Work marchers in the Albert Hall. March 1976

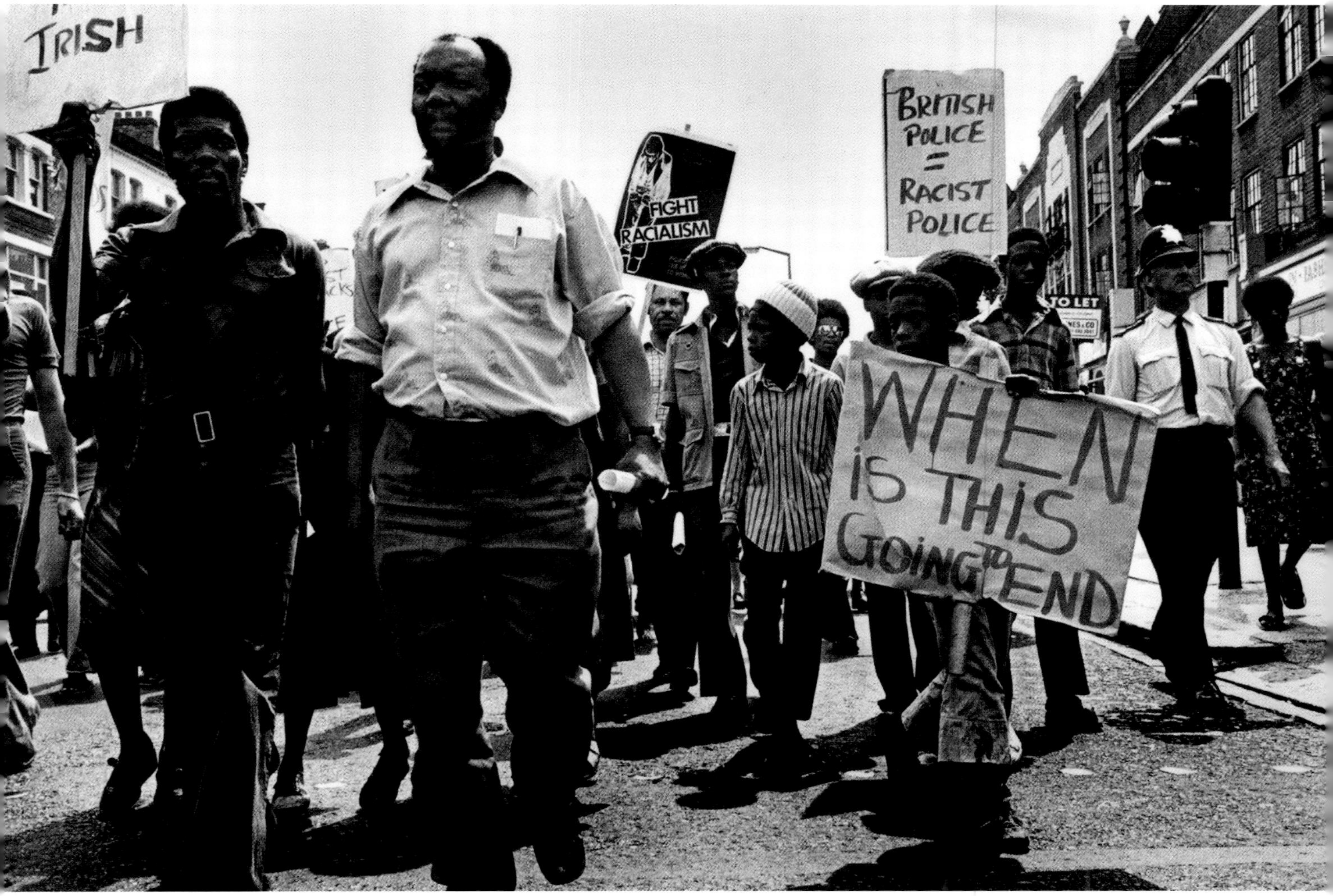

84. Afro-Caribbean march through West London. June 1976

I specialised in still life and then in food in all its aspects:
freshness, abundance, cooking, rotting, celebrating and sharing.
I continued to make portraits and came to understand the meaning
of Stieglitz's extended essay of his lover Georgia O'Keefe:
I photographed my beautiful wife over and over
and finally returned home to my love of documentary
by shooting films.

OLD AGE

OBJECTIVE:

In western social democracies like Great Britain, it is necessary to seem to care for all human beings including the elderly. Since religious ideology and other moral considerations do allow politicians or bureaucrats to consider euthanasia, a veneer of support in old age must be maintained to appear humane. The reality in the 1970s (and it seems still today) is that minimum standards of cleanliness and healthcare are provided by the state. The idea that the old should be honoured, celebrated and provided for in the best possible way is not in the creative or moral vocabulary of the present state. While the Japanese honour their ancestors and there is still a position for the elderly in the extended household of many European countries, the British and Americans hide their senior citizens away in "homes". These abominations give other and more sinister meanings to the word "home". Where do we find the best care in the world? Where are the stimulating programmes of art and entertainment? Where are the nurses and staff to help the tired, sick and dependent? Why are people allowed to spend days alone, in unwelcome solitude, waiting for death? I don't have the answers. Perhaps the reason is that the elderly are no longer net creators of wealth, but rather net consumers.

SUBJECTIVE

I photographed for several weeks in an old people's home in London where most of the residents came from the working class. There were some rare moments of humour and a very little entertainment, of exceedingly poor quality, treating the residents as though they were children. Arguments were frequent – but there were moments of flirting, animated discussions and long, slow descriptions of the most recent illness. It was a place of sadness where the only relief was memory ... and death. A society that under-educates the mass of its children, that worships wealth-creation, that ignores culture, and dismisses its elders to a social and emotional hell, is truly dysfunctional.

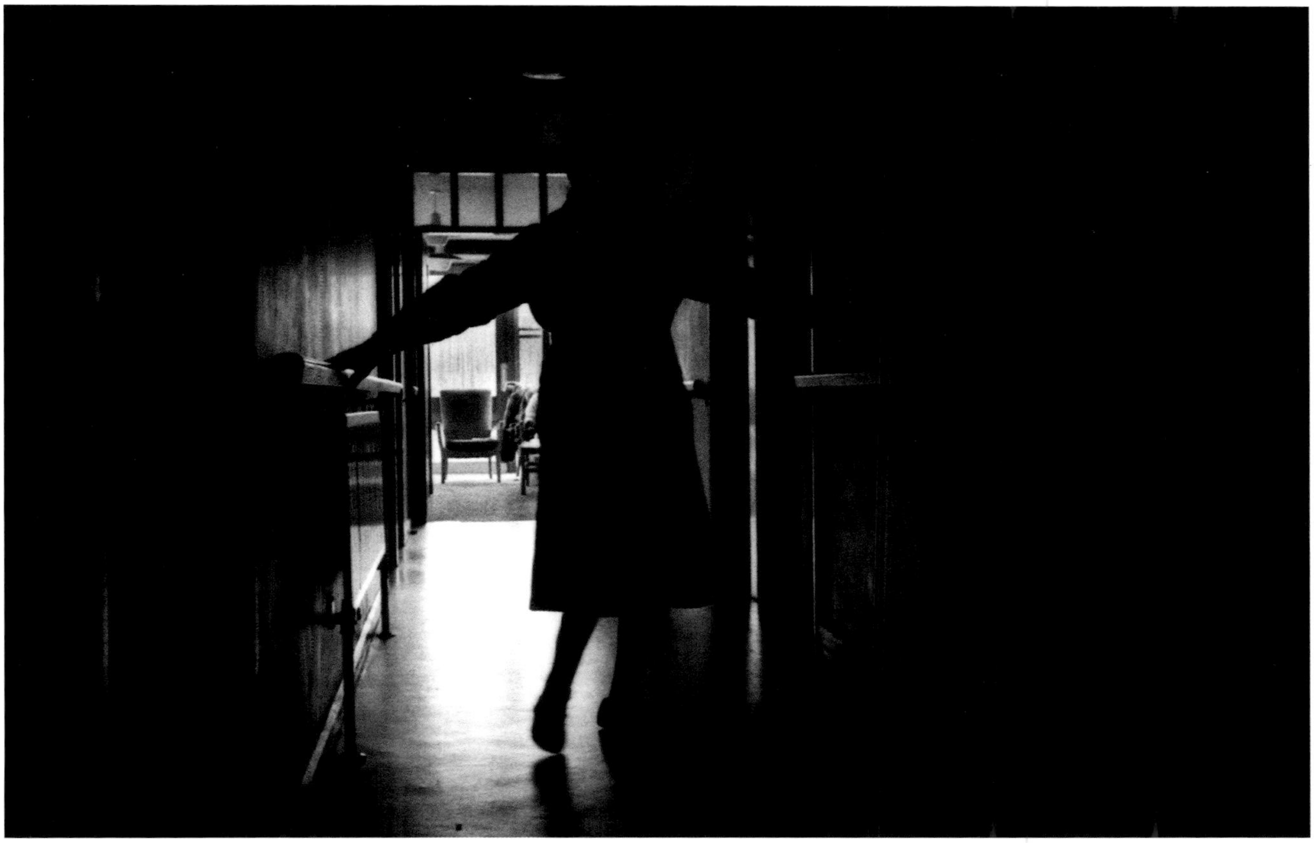

85. Woman in corridor, Old People's Home, London. 1971

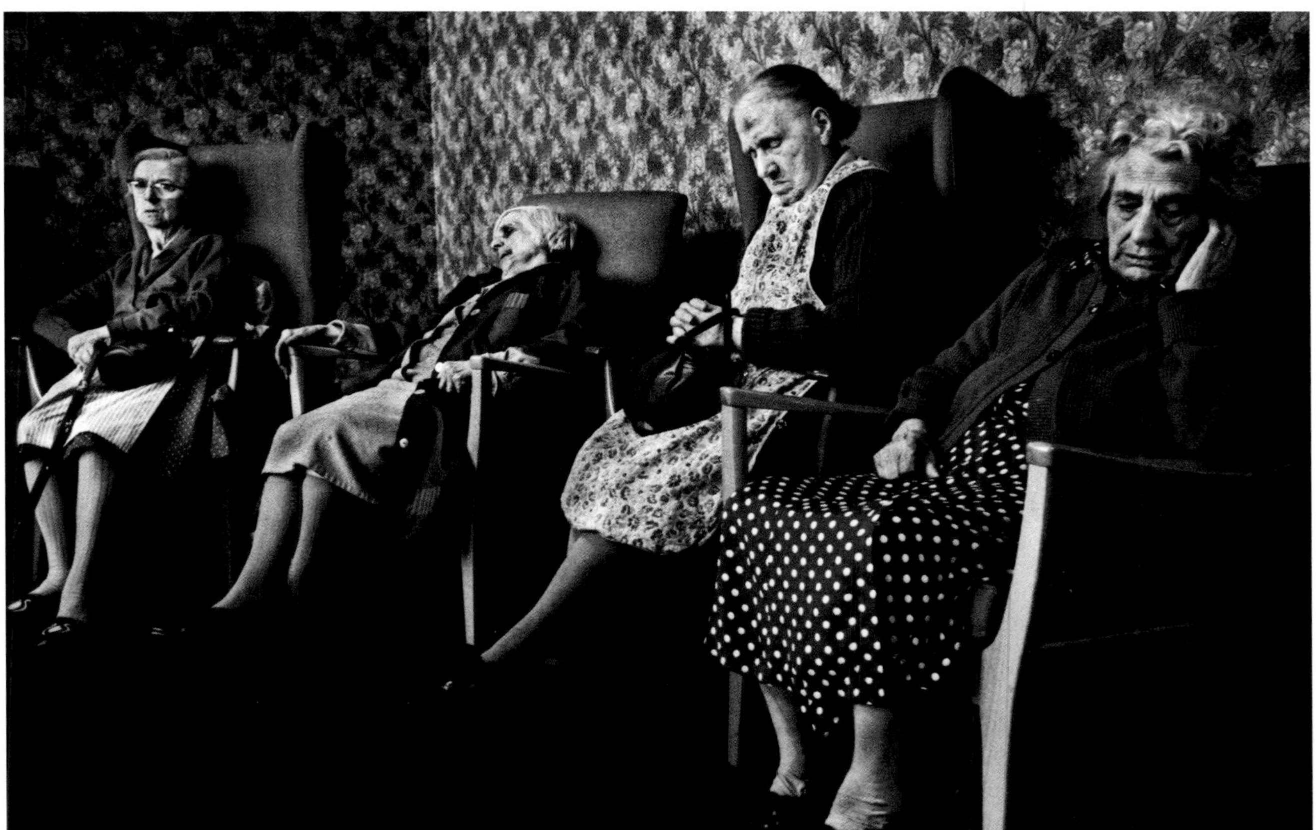

86. Four women waiting, Old People's Home, London. 1971

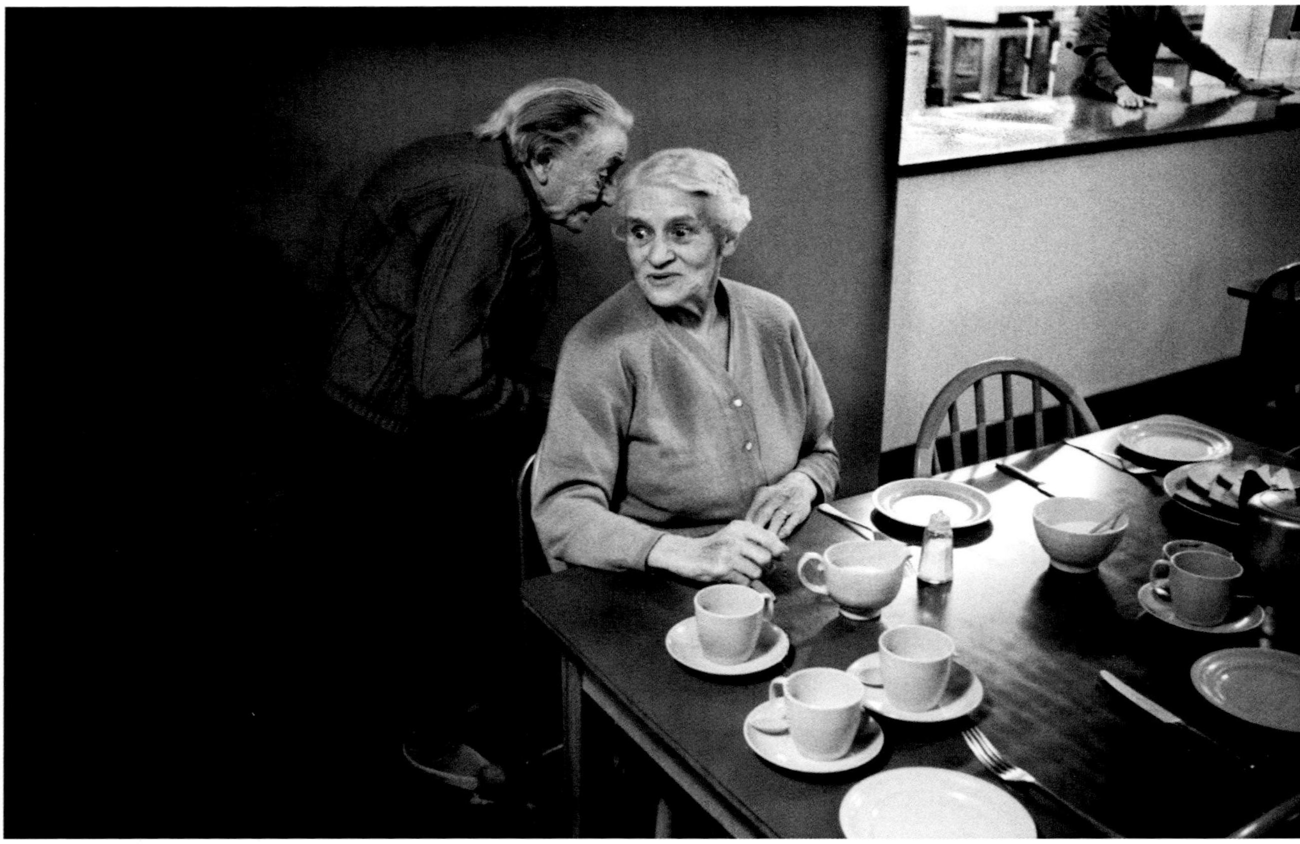

87. Gossip, Old People's Home, London. 1971

Knowledge, love, work, beauty.
I dream of Utopias. I know they are dreams
but I dream of order out of chaos,
warm light rolling across life
as the sun across a Tuscan landscape.
I envision beautiful form, beautiful moments,
glowing faces, hospitable people,
love like a lantern on a hostile road.

88. Woman waits near window, Old People's Home, London. 1971

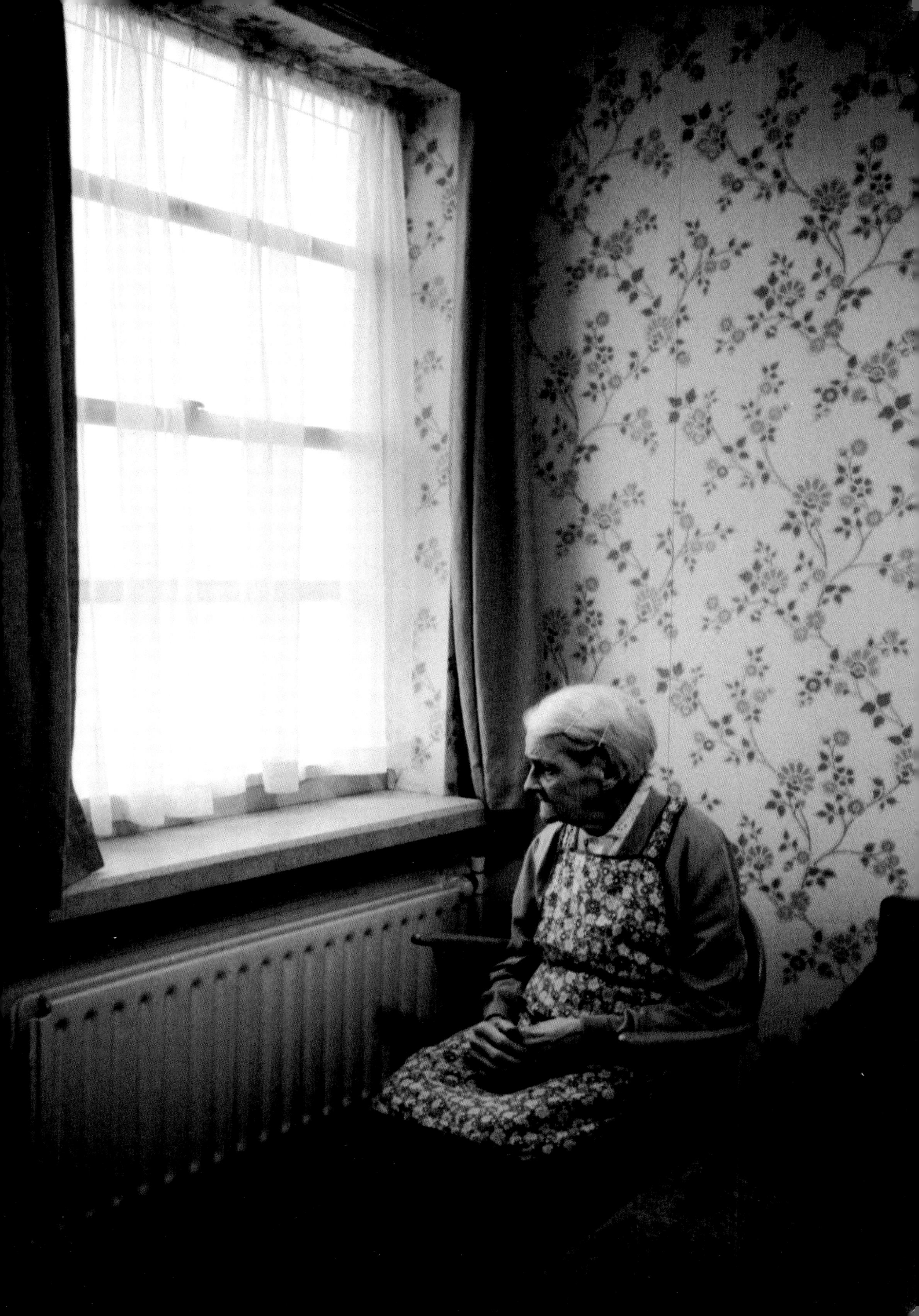

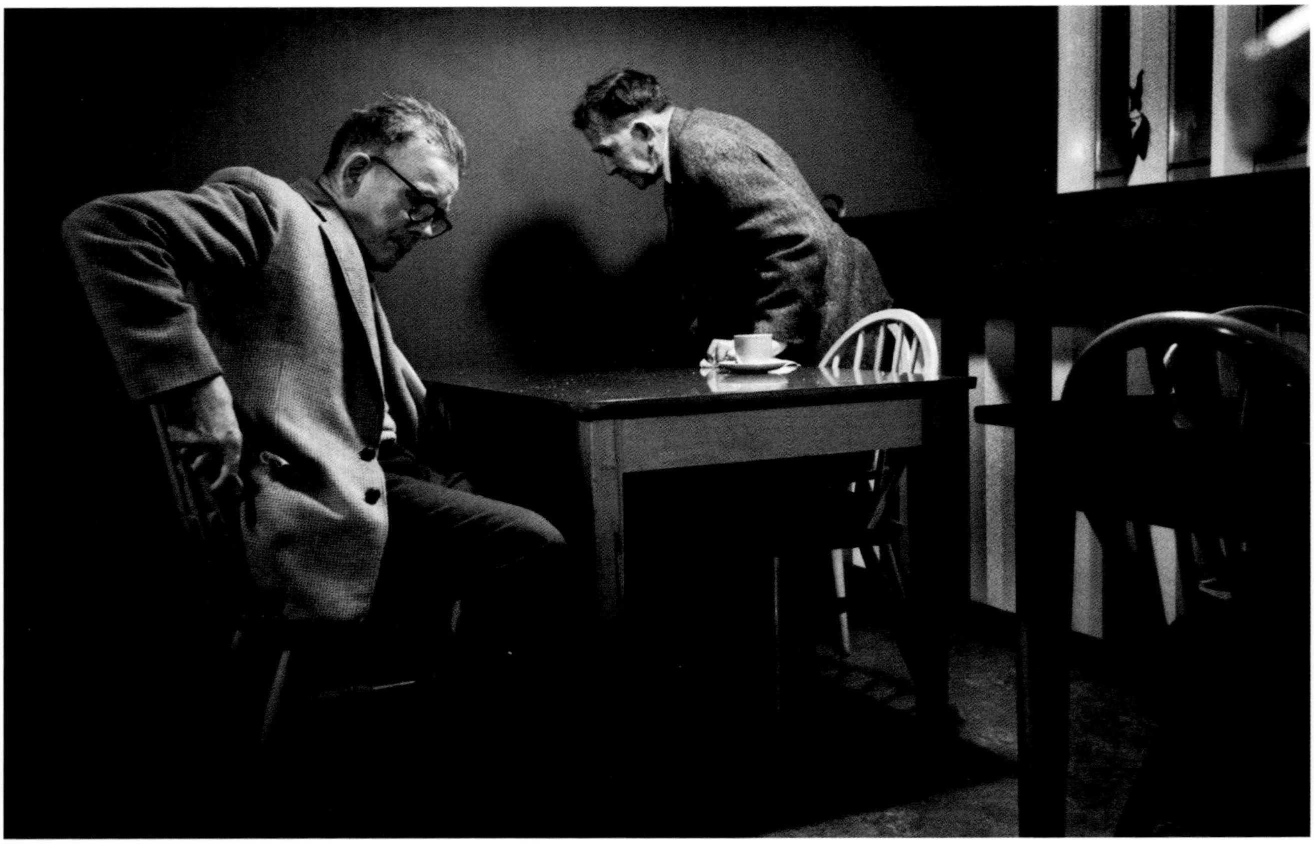

89. Two men, Old People's Home, London. 1971

He quietly walked amongst these people
and he loved them
for those moments he was exposed to them
and for maybe longer.

(text from the script *A Piece of Glass,* about image making, by Robert Golden)

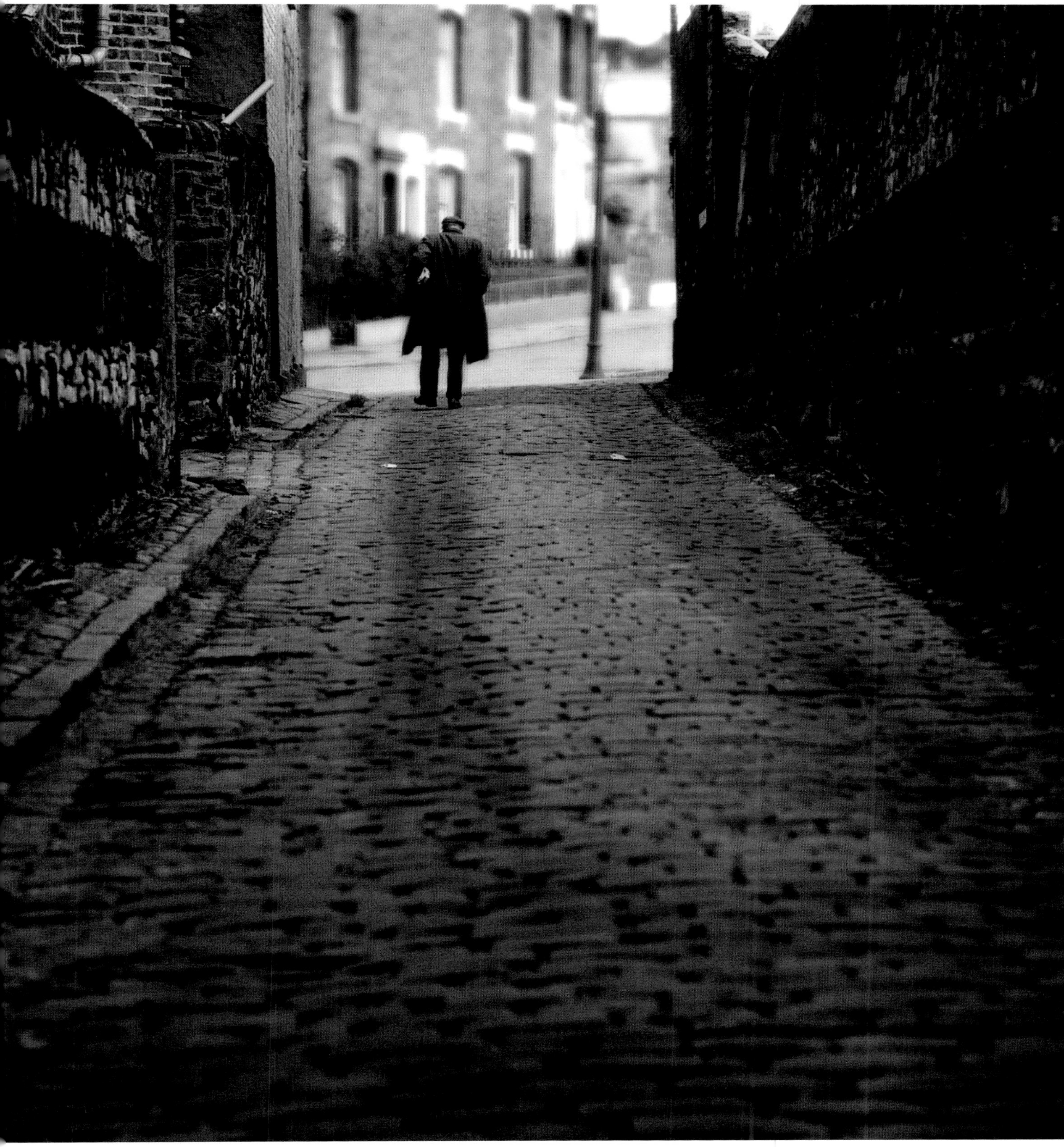

90. Man going home, Bradford. Autumn 1973

THE NEW GLOBALISM

Three hundred corporations directly or indirectly control more than four billion people worldwide involved in growing, processing, transporting and selling food.

Trans-national commodities buyers, international shipping agents, giant food processing corporations, supermarket chains and fast food outlets, along with insurance companies and banks, create huge profits.

Since the demise of the Soviet Union and the creation of a uni-polar world centred in the United States, globalism has developed and spread from the realms of finance and manufacturing into the field of agriculture.

Although this tendency began in the 1960s and 70s, it accelerated in the late 1990s under the neo-cons in the United States with their desire to privatise government and to spread their vision into every area of the world and into every sector of culture. The consequences of this process are that millions of people have been left without education, healthcare, sufficient food – hungry and homeless.

Culture is obliterated under a tsunami of international electronic media. Traditions are swept away as the social fabric of villages and rural communities breaks down. An existential gloom spreads as people feel helpless in the face of changes they do not understand. In the end, farms and villages are abandoned, market towns dwindle and the land is over-taken by trans-national corporations and turned into vast mono-crop estates employing impoverished people at below subsistence wages.

We all hope that this pernicious condition will change under President Obama.

These colour images are screen grabs from a series of documentaries I shot from 2002 to 2004 called SAVOURING EUROPE. They began as a celebration of the wonderful, complex and varied food cultures of Europe. Everywhere I filmed, I realised that people were under threat from winds of change. They could feel the effects but they could not see the origin. This was because the changes originated often thousands of miles away, in boardrooms where decisions were made about commodity purchases, food distribution, advertising and marketing, decisions which had nothing directly to do with the people on the ground in France, or Romania or Britain. I began to see in people's eyes that same fear and sense of dislocation, indeed the creeping dread of loss, particularly the loss of HOME, that I had witnessed years earlier in the industrial areas of Britain. It occurred to me that although I had set out to document a celebration of wonderful riches, I was in fact documenting people's struggles to maintain the customs, traditions and social connections that constitute HOME in the face of this new phase of globalisation.

When studying history I was taught to ask the simple question about any event, especially about an event that remains unclear ... who gains? While the trial of time has not yet been held, I am certain that the answer will always be the corporations and never the people.

FRESHNESS>ABUNDANCE>COOKING>CELEBRATING>SHARING

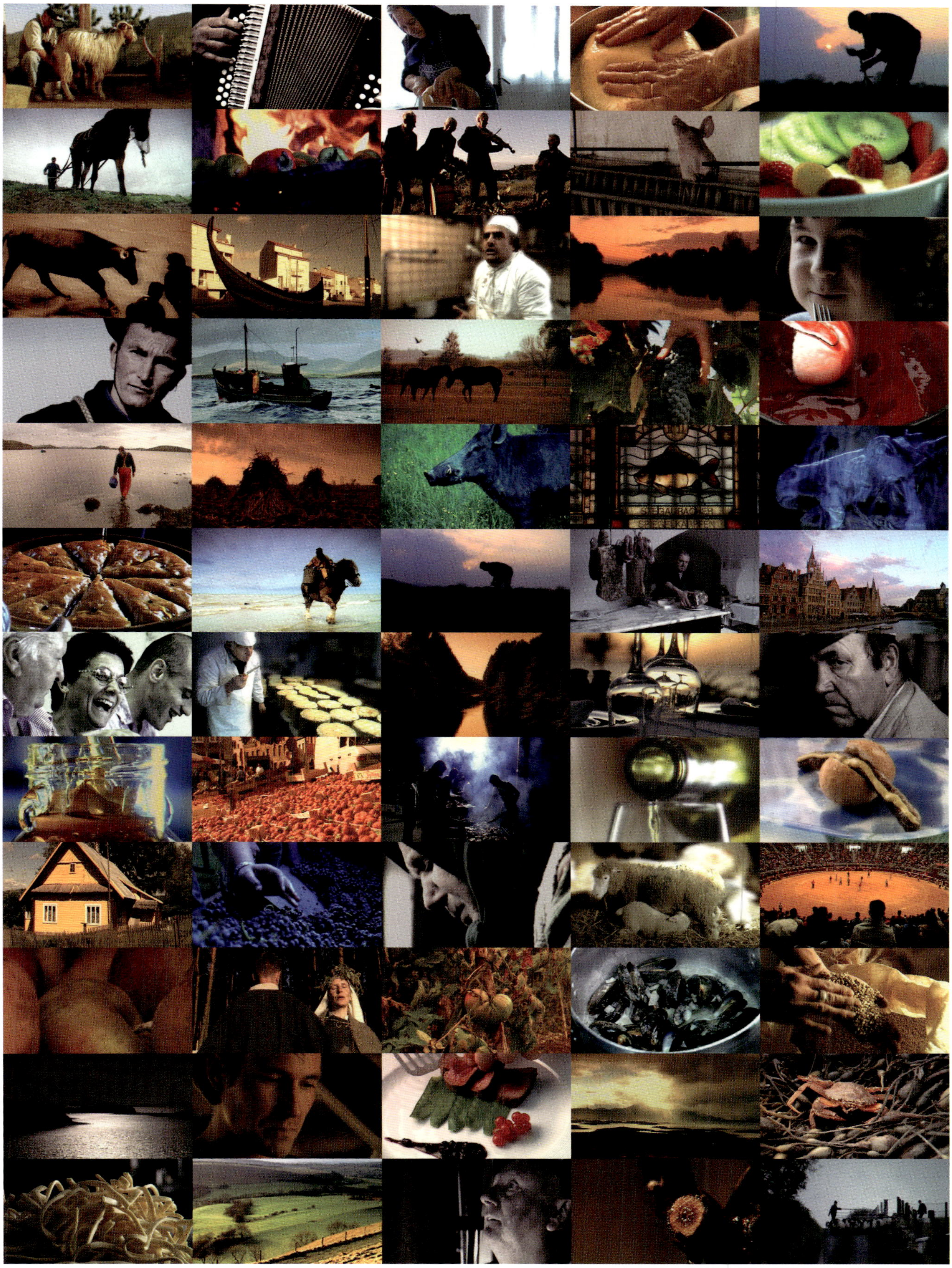

EARTH>GROUND>DIRT>SOIL>HOUSE>HOME

The EARTH is the third planet from the sun.

The EARTH is the fifth largest planet.

The EARTH is a big ball of fiery mud spinning through endless time and space.

The EARTH, according to humans, is the only planet with life on it.

The EARTH is the only planet known to humans that has a biosphere.

A biosphere is a unique and delicate combination of matter capable of supporting life.

Some say that while the sky refers to life, the EARTH represents dead, unconscious matter. Others say the sky is our father and the earth is our mother.

In some symbolic systems Mother EARTH is womb and tomb.

"Nothing lives long, only the EARTH and the mountains"
Cheyenne death song

"The EARTH" refers to the planet as opposed to earth as ground.

The WORLD is another word to describe the EARTH.

The outer WORLD is large and we experience it through our senses. When we close our eyes we imagine or remember an inner WORLD.

"We must not use the WORLD as if we created it ourselves."
From THE GIFT OF A GOOD LAND by Wendell Berry

LAND may refer to the part of the earth that is not covered by water.

LAND is also a synonym for a region belonging to a people; a country, a geographical area that connotes an independent political entity; a nation, particularly in the absence of a state or government; Motherland, Fatherland, and homeland, a person's country of affiliation, birth or ancestral origin.
From Wikipedia

The ability to endure on the LAND exists for as long as people do not break their bond with it. This is for as long as they submit to it as opposed to making it submit to them.

Tragedy lies in the path of industrialising and profiteering from our LAND. This is the curse of people with vision but without the ability to see what is in front of them.
Paraphrased from THE GIFT OF A GOOD EARTH by Wendell Berry

The dead bequeathed the LAND to the living and to the unborn of the living. The living, to be good parents and neighbours, must be responsible to do the same.
Paraphrased from THE GIFT OF A GOOD EARTH by Wendell Berry

"We do not own the LAND, we borrow it from our children"
A native North American proverb

GROUND refers to the surface of the earth or to a combination of sand and organic matter found on the surface of the earth.

SOIL is among our most important natural resources because of its position in the landscape and its dynamic, physical, chemical, and biological functions.

SOIL is a live medium. The better the SOIL the better the crops. The better the crops the better the food. The better the food the healthier the person.

"If a man loves the SOIL he will save it." *Henry Besuden*

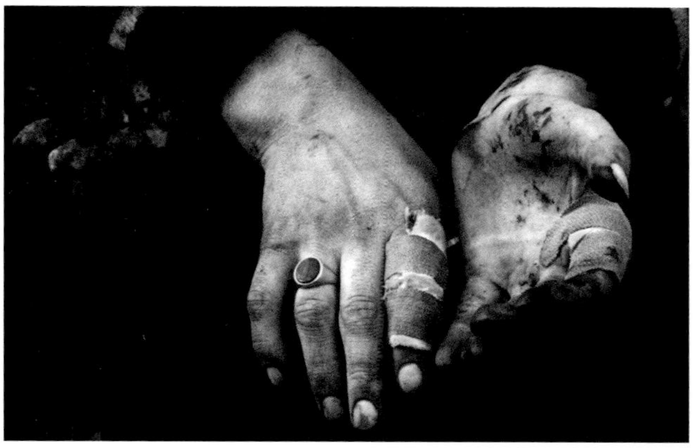

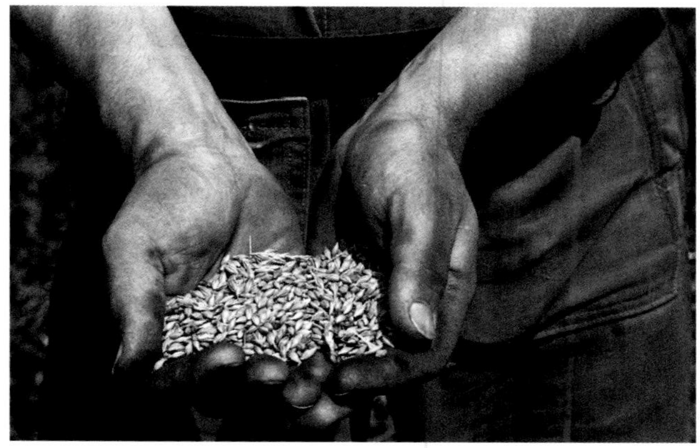

DIRT may refer to soil or the ground.

DIRT often means waste material, an unwanted or undesired mixture of dust, soil and other solids.

DIRT therefore may imply a lifeless soil, something used up, brought to ruin and unwanted.

People in North America may be referred to as DIRT poor.

When the rich topsoil, which took millennia to create, is overworked and laid waste by artificial fertilisers or poisoned by pesticides and other industrially-based chemicals, that topsoil becomes DIRT, a nutritionless dead matter useful only for holding rather than feeding root systems.

DWELLINGS usually sit on, but sometimes are dug into the earth or they may be in caves or trees.

DWELLING, as well as being a term for a house or for living somewhere, or for lingering somewhere – is a philosophical concept which was developed by Martin Heidegger. He meant it as "being-in-the-world".

HOUSE is another word for dwelling, usually referring to a specific structure.

A HOUSE in dreams often represents the ego or self.

A HOUSE in dreams often represents family life, a place where one may be happy and safe.

The average American HOUSE now has 190 square metres of floor space, up by 90 per cent since the 1950s. Yet because individuals now move 14 times in a lifetime, there are fewer opportunities to accrue memories of a HOUSE.

"Memories do not add a dollar to the value of your house, yet these are the very things that comprise real value ... and create the sense of HOME."
Paraphrased from David Suzuki

The concept of HOME is broader than a physical dwelling.

A HOME is a place where a person or family lives, perhaps spends much of their time, or where a person is comfortable.

HOME is often a place of refuge and safety, where worldly cares fade and the things and people that one loves become the focus.

Some people think of HOME as when they grew up ... a time rather than a place.

The opposite of HOME as "a place of time, memory and happiness" is HOME as where one does not want to be, because one believes that it is in other places where good things happen.

A good HOME is bad for business.
In a good HOME people are happy and healthy.
In a bad HOME, where there is strife, there will be unease and therefore expensive prescription or recreational drugs.
Or there may be dis-ease and therefore more drugs.
And if the bad HOME is broken, there are then two unhappy HOMES, each reliant on drugs and cars and petrol and separate white goods ... more sales, more business, more profits.
A good HOME is bad for business.
Paraphrased from THE GIFT OF A GOOD LAND by Wendell Berry

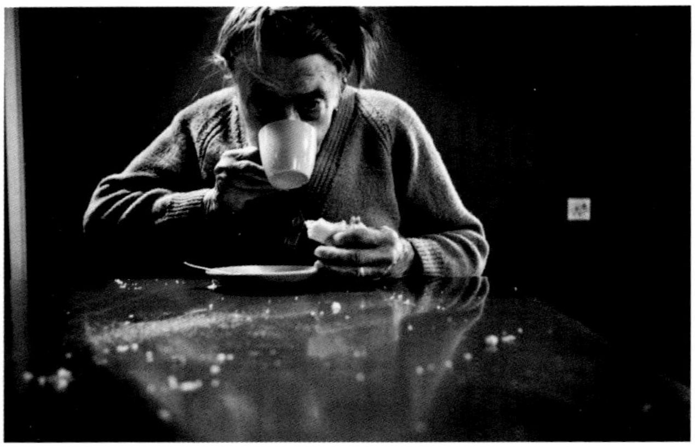

ACKNOWLEDGMENTS

The original exhibition would not have happened without the foresight, creative thinking and support of Jem Main of the Study Gallery of Modern Art (now KUBE) in Poole Dorset.

Neither the exhibition's journey to Frome nor this book of the exhibition would have happened without the inspired and dogged work of Jacqueline Peverely.

And not much I do would connect with the world if it were not for the endless inspiration, lateral thinking, diplomatic skills and general loving support of my wife Tina.

Thanks to Fanny Charles and Gay Pirrie-Weir.

Finally I want to express my gratitude to Felix Dennis and to Butler Tanner and Dennis for their active help and support in printing this book.

Designed by Louise Leffler

All photographs and film clips by Robert Golden